Annie's
Easy Treats

Annie's
Easy Treats

Anne Mayne and Diane Simmonds

Kangaroo Press

Acknowledgments

Putting this book together would not have been possible without the help and support of the following friends who supplied recipes, including some old family secrets!

Shirley Althofer, Libby Birch, Nana Bess Broadley, Lorraine Dolanski, Eileen Freeman, Yvonne Griffiths, 'Lolly Wishes' of Blackheath, Janet Prince, Muriel, Jeneen, Beth and Kylie Simmonds, and Elsie Winter. We also wish to thank our families who gave their opinions at various 'Treat Tastings' and refrained from eating all the goodies before they were photographed.

Our Mudgee photographer, Michael Coates, again did a terrific job.

© Anne Mayne and Diane Simmonds 1994

First published in 1994 by Kangaroo Press Pty Ltd
3 Whitehall Road Kenthurst NSW 2156 Australia
PO Box 6125 Dural Delivery Centre NSW 2158
Typeset by G.T. Setters Pty Limited
Printed in Hong Kong through Colorcraft Ltd

ISBN 0 86417 618 X

Contents

INTRODUCTION   7

PACKAGING AND PRESENTATION   8

CONVERSION TABLES   10

1. Chocolate Treats   11
Basic Dipping Mix   11
Chocolate Cherries   11
Chocolate Ginger   12
Chocolate Prunes with Port   12
Easy Homemade Chocolates   12
Apricot Ambrosia   13
Chocolate Spiders   13
Fruity Frosts   13
French Chocolates   14

2. Cereal Treats   15
Honey Bubble Crunch   15
Weet-Bix Kids   15
Cereal Cases   16
Chocolate Roughs   16
Cherry Coconut Bars   17
Bubbly Marshmallows   17
Pink Mallow Bars   17
Honey Joys   18

3. Favourite Treats   19
Toffee and Toffee Testing   19
Butterscotch   20
Barley Sugar   20
Umbrella Toffees and School Toffees   20
Toffee Apples   25
Popcorn—Basic Recipe   25
Candy Popcorn   26
Caramel Popcorn   26
Coconut Ice   26
Chocolate Crackles   27
Sherbet   27
Honeycomb   27

4. Sweet Treats   28
Moonshine Biffs   28
Easy Rocky Road   28
Apricot Surprises   28
Marzipan Log   29
Peanut Butter Balls   29
Sesame Caramel Toffee   30
Pine Nut Toffees   30
Sesame Snaps   30

5. Kids' Treats   31
Packaging Ideas   31
Truccles   34
Strawberries   34
Edible Animals   34
Marzipan Animals and Shapes   35
Marshmallow   35
  Marshmallow Cones   35
  Marshmallow Cups   35
Smartie Squares   36
Funny Faces   36
Gingerbread Men   36

6. Snack Treats   41
Carrot Candies   41
Apricot Rounds   41
Date Slices   42
Muesli Bars   42
Candied Peel   43
Muesli Munchies   43
Peanut Butter Squares   43

7. Savoury Treats   44
Caraway Sticks   44
Nutty Nibbles   44
Curried Nuts and Bolts   45
Cheese Rounds   45
Devilled Raisins   45
Herb Twists   46
Chilli Nuts   46
Pizza Popcorn   46

8. Nutty Treats   48
Nutty Honey Chews   48
Orange Sugared Pecans   48
Sugar Coated Peanuts   49
Ginger Peanut Toffee   49
Creamy Peanut Balls   49
Coffee Pecans   50

9. Fudge and Nougat Treats   51
Chocolate Fudge   51
Cherry Bars   51
Peanut Butter Fudge   52
Cream Cheese Fudge   52
Coconut Walnut Fudge   52
Cherry Divinity   53
Golden Caramels   53

10. Slice and Bar Treats   54
Apricot Delight   54
Walnut Slice   54
Cocoa Peanut Logs   55

Sesame Honey Fingers   55
Basic Slice   55
Macadamia Slice   56
Sultana Slice   56
Marshmallow Slice   56
Caramel Slice   61

11. Celebration Treats   62
Santa's Special Buttons   62
White Christmas   62
Fruit Cake Rum Balls   63
Christmas Crunch   63
Mini Christmas Puddings   64
Christmas Logs   64
Mini Christmas Cakes   64
Christmas Parcels   65
Easter Bonnets   65
Chocolate Easter Eggs   66
Liqueur Easter Eggs   66

INDEX   67

Introduction

This book gathers together a collection of delicious recipes for all kinds of different sweet and savoury treats. With the emphasis on 'easy to make' at little expense, even the most inexperienced cook will be able to make a selection of the most delectable treats.

These are ideal recipes for packaging up to sell at fetes, fundraising events, on market stalls or through other outlets for a bit of extra cash. There are many special occasions throughout the year to sell such treats. Mother's Day is an ideal time for lots of delicious goodies prettily packaged. Kids can help make and package up all kinds of interesting savoury nibblies for Father's Day. Families can enjoy making and giving special treats at Easter and Christmas time, and decorate them accordingly. Everyone enjoys the thought that goes with a handmade gift.

Take along some homemade chocolates, wrapped and presented attractively, to your hostess at your next dinner party outing to have with coffee. You can make a range of homemade treats that store well in airtight jars on your shelf or in your refrigerator, so you will always have something on hand should guests drop by unexpectedly.

Most of the recipes in this book use ingredients that are fairly standard in most households. They include suggestions on the number of items that can be made from each recipe, on storage and on packaging.

The book is broken up into eleven different categories of Treats, such as 'Chocolate Treats' with lots of mouth-watering recipes for chocoholics, 'Cereal Treats' which uses many different types of cereals as a base for each recipe, and 'Favourite Treats' with many of the old time favourites which will always be popular. 'Sweet Treats' will appeal to the sweet tooth in the family, and the 'Kids' Treats' section has a range of colourful and interesting recipes the children will just love to help make!

'Snack Treats' with tasty squares, slices and bars with all kinds of healthy ingredients will be great to pack for lunches or picnics or to package and sell as a tasty treat. 'Savoury Treats' will be popular with the menfolk as there are all kinds of nibblies such as popcorn, nuts, raisins, pretzels and more. 'Nutty Treats' have a range of recipes, all with a nutty flavour.

The 'Fudge and Nougat' section has a mouth-watering selection, and 'Slice and Bar Treats' are always popular and good sellers. The Christmas and Celebration section gives lots of ideas for making and decorating treats for special occasions and gifts.

We have also compiled a helpful guide on cooking tips, with conversion tables, and setting temperatures for various stages of cookery. Another section has been devoted to packaging and presentation ideas for selling these various treats which will be helpful for groups making many treats in bulk to sell for fundraising purposes.

There are lots of hints throughout the book for presenting and varying the recipes which you will find useful.

We are confident you will enjoy making many of the delicious sweet and savoury recipes in this book, as we have enjoyed making and compiling them for you to try! Armed with the recipes from *Annie's Easy Treats* you are sure to find your next fundraising event, market stall or gift giving a huge success!

Packaging and Presentation

Packaging is so important to the overall look of homemade treats. If the presentation is as enticing as the treats themselves, you are sure to sell your goods. Plates 32, 33 and 34 illustrate some of the ideas in this section.

Packaging

There are so many different ways to enhance the packaging of your treats, not only by the use of purchased items such as colourful patty cases and foil chocolate cases, cellophane and generous amounts of gift ribbon, but also by the imaginative use of lots of free recycled bits and pieces which are easily collected. This is especially important for groups wishing to keep their costs down and their profits up!

Simple ideas for packaging many of the Easy Treats in this book, many using recycled materials which are readily available, include:

• **Jars** Small jars with lids can be used for smaller sweets, with the added benefit that storing them in an airtight jar means you are assured they will remain fresh until sale day. Try dressing up the jars with circles of pretty fabric with pinked edges—ideal for Mother's Day. Tie up with gift ribbon, which is inexpensive, with the ends curled attractively. You can also attach a handmade label using coloured cardboard or handmade paper. (Glass jars are not suitable for very small children to take home as a gift for Mum as there is always the risk of breakage.)

• **Baskets** Small baskets in a variety of shapes can often be purchased very inexpensively at discount stores or market stalls. They can be filled with a variety of treats and packaged up in colourful cellophane. You may wish to line the basket with a paper napkin or a paper doily. Tie up the bundle in the basket with generous amounts of gift ribbon to decorate.

• **Cardboard** Coloured cardboard can be put to a variety of uses. Children will have fun cutting out and fashioning simple basket shapes. Use a stapler to hold the basket together and to attach both ends of the basket handle. Fill with sweets wrapped in cellophane. See instructions in Kids' Treats, page 31.

To make a cardboard cone first cut out a circle approximately 20 cm (8'') in diameter and then cut it in half. Overlap the straight edges of each semi circle and staple in place to make a cone shape for sweets. Children might also like to decorate the baskets and cones with coloured Texta pens, glue and glitter. With the addition of a ribbon or a cardboard loop the cone can be hung on a Christmas tree.

• **Boxes** Save small boxes of different shapes. Use colourful gift paper to cover the boxes to store sweets. Tie up with gift ribbon like a parcel with a bow for a special surprise. Even lids such as shoe box lids can be utilised. Cover them with gift paper or even wallpaper samples. As they are shallow they can be used to present single layers of treats. Cover treats by stretching over and sticky taping plastic wrap or cellophane in place on the bottom of the box lid.

• **Tins** Recycled tins can be painted with acrylic household paint, or covered with wallpaper, gift wrap or Contact paper, and filled with sweets. You can either package up the tin and contents in cellophane, or present the sweets in a plastic or cellophane bag tied up with gift ribbon and pushed down into the decorated tin.

• **Takeaway containers** Chinese takeaway containers, round or oblong with lids, can be very useful as they are airtight. Ensure everything is thoroughly clean if recycling packaging materials. Children might like to cut up old cards and glue different motifs to the lids for special occasions such as Christmas or Father's Day.

• **Ties** Goodies can be packaged up in lots of different ways and some of the things you can use to tie up the packages are inexpensive gift ribbon, raffia, ribbon, and thick wool.

• **Bags** Plastic or cellophane bags can be very useful. They have the advantage of being very inexpensive, come in a variety of sizes, are quickly filled, and show off the treats through the clear packaging. Decorate the bags with curled gift ribbon, thick wool, Papertwist ribbon bows, stickers and handmade labels. Some items may be presented flat on a piece of cardboard covered in foil as a base. Wholesalers have a wide array of packaging materials available, if you cannot purchase through a stationery shop or newsagent.

You can also make your own bags from giftwrap paper; kids love these clever little gift bags. They are also a great idea for children to make themselves to help raise funds for their school fete, church group or fundraising venture. Directions are set out in 'Kids' Treats' on page 33.

• **Glasses and Mugs** Package up sweets in an attractive glass or coffee mug, wrapped and decorated with cellophane and ribbons. They make great gift ideas, being re-usable long after the sweets are gone. A more inexpensive idea is to utilise plastic catering cups and wine glasses in the same way.

There are more ideas on packaging treats for children in the 'Kids' Treats' section. They are perfect for birthday parties, sweets stalls at fetes and will be a huge success with the kids at your next market day!

There are many ways to package treats to make them more presentable, such as winding gift ribbon around toffee apple sticks and curling the ends prettily. You are sure to have lots of fun making them as attractive as possible, whether for sale or for gift giving—all it takes is a little imagination!

Presentation

Presentation of your attractively packaged goods is very important! If your stall or table looks inviting, people will be drawn to it to look at your goods. Cover your table in a pretty cloth, perhaps with a lace overlay (a large colourful sheet and lace curtaining can be utilised). Use an umbrella for shade, blow up some colourful balloons, and use fresh flowers and pretty ribbons to dress up your table.

If your stall is geared towards children, you can use teddy bears, dolls and toys as props, lots of bright primary colours, and masses of colourful balloons to attract them. Have someone dress up as a clown to promote your stall and add to the fun of the day. Make sure there are plenty of inexpensive items for children to buy with their pocket money. Toffee apples, marshmallow in cones, sherbet bags, bags of popcorn, chocolate crackles and so on are always favourites with the kids.

For Mother's Day, use vases of fresh flowers, lots of ribbons and pretty pastel shades to appeal. Chocolates, fudges and other sweet treats will be very acceptable gifts.

For an old-fashioned stall selling all the long-time favourite sweets, try small granny print fabrics as jar toppers, a few antique items such as an old balance scale, and dress for the part in an old world outfit, pinny and bonnet! You might also like to have a row of glass candy jars so people can make their own selection of their old-

time favourites. (Just as they did in the olden days!)

For a more masculine look for Father's Day, use hessian to cover your table, and decorations in brown, navy, green, tartan, spots or stripes. You can also use a sporting or bush theme for your table. Do up bags of Curried Nuts and Bolts, Pizza Popcorn and other great nibblies for dads. Don't forget Australian gumnuts and dried flowers as a decoration or garnish for the tourists to your area, especially for recipes containing macadamia nuts, for instance.

A good fundraising idea is to gather together a wide selection of the most delectable treats, all beautifully packaged in a big basket for a raffle. You may find you get further orders from other groups and charities to make up baskets for their raffles too.

Fundraising committees will find lots of these ideas helpful to ensure the success of the next fete or charity event.

If you are interested in making a bit of extra income, an obvious place to sell is at your local market. The busiest times will be at Easter, Mother's Day and Christmas. Old favourites like coconut ice, marshmallows, honeycomb and toffees will always be popular. Include more luxurious treats such as fudges and chocolates for variety. You should ensure your treats are fresh and packaged appropriately.

Your local council or tourist office can also advise the dates of local festivals where large crowds are expected which may be worthwhile attending. Approach charity organisations and let them know you can make up a basket of special treats for use in a raffle.

Approaching local stores in your area to take goods for sale may also be of benefit. Craft and gift stores are logical outlets, and you can make it known you are willing to make up gift baskets of sweets for special occasions. Treats which do not require refrigeration and can be packaged for some time are the best items to sell in this way. You should also see if any of your local restaurants or hotels are interested in taking some savoury treats as appetisers, or chocolates and fudges for after-dinner treats with coffee.

To calculate how much each treat costs to make, add up the costs of the ingredients used, and divide by the number of bars, slices, squares, balls, etc. you end up with. This will give you an indication of how much you should charge to make a reasonable profit. Some ingredients will be more expensive than others and you should charge appropriately.

Again, careful packaging and presentation of the sweet or savoury treats ensure they look delicious and are highly saleable, guaranteeing the success of your next marketing venture.

Conversion Tables

(Australian Standard Measures)

Direct conversion to imperial measurements of volume from metric measurements is extremely difficult. Metric equivalents are approximately 10% more than the imperial measurements.

Measure	Metric	Imperial
cup	250 ml	8 fl. oz (227 ml)
tablespoon	20 ml	½ fl. oz (14.2 ml)
teaspoon	5 ml	⅛ fl. oz (3.6 ml)

There is no Australian standard dessertspoon measurement.

Conversion of Liquids and Cup Measures

Imperial and Metric Cup	Millilitres	Imperial
	30 ml	1 fl. oz
¼ cup	85 ml	2 fl. oz
⅓ cup	100 ml	3 fl. oz
½ cup		4 fl. oz
	150 ml	5 fl. oz (¼ pint)
¾ cup		6 fl. oz
1 cup	250 ml	8 fl. oz
1¼ cups		10 fl. oz (½ pint)
1½ cups	375 ml	12 fl. oz
1¾ cups		14 fl. oz
2 cups	500 ml	16 fl. oz
2½ cups	625 ml	20 fl. oz (1 pint)
4 cups	1 litre	32 fl. oz
5 cups	1.25 litres	40 fl. oz (2 pints)

Conversion of Masses

Grams	Ounces
15 g	½ oz
30 g	1 oz
60 g	2 oz
90 g	3 oz
125 g	4 oz (¼ lb)
155 g	5 oz
185 g	6 oz
220 g	7 oz
250 g	8 oz (½ lb)
280 g	9 oz
315 g	10 oz
345 g	11 oz
375 g	12 oz (¾ lb)
410 g	13 oz
440 g	14 oz
470 g	15 oz
500 g	16 oz (1 lb)

Oven Temperature Conversion

The number of degrees Celsius is approximately half the number of degrees Fahrenheit.

Description	°Celsius	°Fahrenheit
Cool	100	200
	110	225
Very slow	120	250
	140	275
Slow	150	300
Moderately slow	160	325
Moderate	180	350
Moderately hot	190	375
	200	400
Hot	220	425
	230	450
Very hot	250	475
	260	500

1. Chocolate Treats

We could write a whole book on chocolate! Nothing sells better than chocolate—the food of romantics and the gods. The best time to sell chocolates at a fete or market stall is in the cooler months as you don't need to worry about high temperatures. If chocolates are subjected to heat or left in the hot sun, they can melt, discolour and lose their shiny appearance. It is also best not to store them in the refrigerator as in extreme cold they are inclined to sweat and lose their glossy appearance. Chocolates keep well in an airtight container or packaged up in bags for sale.

You can do virtually anything that tantalises your taste buds with chocolate, so use your imagination! Dip and coat things such as fruit, chunks of ginger, peel, nuts, coconut, marzipans, fondants, toffees, truffle balls, rum balls, coconut balls, and so on. Drain to a smooth finish and then decorate with chocolate swirls, feather and fan designs in either the same chocolate or white chocolate or a contrast.

Also remember white chocolate can be used as a substitute in recipes for colour contrast or variation, or for people who are allergic to ordinary chocolate.

There are so many ways to flavour chocolate—you can use a variety of liqueurs flavoured with orange, mint or coffee, orange or almond essences, rum, brandy, sherry—the list is endless.

Always melt chocolate over barely simmering water in a double saucepan to keep it free of steam or drops of water (as this will thicken and spoil the chocolate). Add Copha to the melting chocolate if you wish to thin it for dipping or coating purposes (as set out in the Basic Dipping Mix below). If you wish to use butter in a recipe, use unsalted butter (*not* margarine) for the best results.

Concentrate on the smell of the finished product as well as the appearance. It should smell enticing as well as look delicious.

Basic Dipping Mix

This is an excellent runny chocolate mixture ideal for dipping or coating purposes.

You will need:
    125 g (4 oz) dark cooking chocolate, chopped
    30 g (1 oz) Copha, chopped

Melt chocolate and Copha over simmering water in a double saucepan. When completely melted, dip different items in the mixture to coat using two forks or toothpicks.

Chocolate Cherries

Glace cherries are soaked in cherry liqueur, rum or port for extra flavour and then coated with chocolate.

You will need:
    100 g (3½ oz) whole glace cherries
    cherry liqueur, rum or port for soaking
    basic dipping mix
    toothpicks

Soak glace cherries overnight in liqueur, rum or port, and drain on absorbent paper. Stick a toothpick in each cherry and dip into chocolate to coat. Place on foil until set. Store in an airtight container. Makes 25. *Plate 2*

11

Chocolate Ginger

Pieces of preserved ginger are extra special covered with chocolate and garnished with a sliver of ginger.

You will need:
   125 g (4 oz) preserved or glazed ginger pieces
   basic dipping mix

Chop preserved ginger or glazed ginger into chunks. Reserve some pieces for garnish and cut into slivers. Dip into melted chocolate using two forks. Garnish with a sliver of ginger. Store in an airtight container. Makes approximately 20. *Plate 4*

Chocolate Prunes with Port

Prunes will never be the same once you have tasted them soaked in port, stuffed with marzipan and dipped in chocolate.

You will need:
   200 g (6½ oz) ready-pitted prunes (approx. 36)
   ½ cup port or rum
   2 tablespoons castor sugar
   100 g (3½ oz) marzipan
   basic dipping mix

Soak prunes overnight in mixture of rum and castor sugar. Drain well on absorbent paper. Knead marzipan well, roll into long sausage shapes, and cut into prune-length sections. Make a slit in each prune and stuff with marzipan. Dip one end of each prune in basic dipping mix. Place on foil or baking paper lined tray in refrigerator to set. Best to keep refrigerated. Makes 36. *Plate 1*

Easy Homemade Chocolates

These chocolates are so quick and easy to make, with only two ingredients, and are great fillers for bags or packaged chocolates.

You will need:
   375 g (12 oz) dark or milk chocolate
   375 g (12 oz) mixed fruit

Melt chocolate in double boiler over simmering heat. Add whole packet of mixed fruit and mix until all ingredients are well coated. Drop teaspoonfuls onto a greased or paperlined baking tray. Allow to set in refrigerator. Store in an airtight jar, or package in cellophane or plastic bags to sell. Makes 36 large or 5 small. *Plate 1*

Apricot Ambrosia

Apricot Ambrosia balls can be half dipped in chocolate, or completely covered—either way, they are delicious!

You will need:
    2 cups Rice Bubbles
    2 cups coconut
    ½ cup sultanas
    1 cup dried apricots, finely chopped
    400 g (1¼ cups) sweetened condensed milk
    375 g (12 oz) chocolate

Place Rice Bubbles, coconut, sultanas and dried apricots in a bowl and blend evenly. Add sweetened condensed milk and mix thoroughly. Roll into balls. Place in a single layer in foil-lined tray and refrigerate until firm.

Melt chocolate over simmering water in a double saucepan. Dip balls into chocolate with two forks, or spear on a toothpick. Dip half the apricot ball in chocolate, or cover completely. Drain and place back onto tray to cool. You can leave them plain, or decorate with chopped nuts, fine strips of glace apricot or chocolate drizzles and swirls. Place in small foil patty papers if desired. Store in an airtight container. Makes 40 large or 50 small. *Plate 1*

Chocolate Spiders

Chocolate Spiders are super easy to make with a distinctive peanutty flavour.

You will need:
    200 g (6½ oz) chocolate
    2 tablespoons crunchy peanut butter
    100 g (3½ oz) packet Chinese fried noodles

Melt chocolate and crunchy peanut butter over simmering hot water in a double saucepan. Add noodles and blend well. Place teaspoonfuls onto a greaseproof paper-lined tray and refrigerate to set. Store in an airtight container. Makes 24. *Plate 1*

Fruity Frosts

Similar to Chocolate Spiders but using white chocolate, dried apricots, almonds and coconut for a unique taste.

Chocolate Spiders

Fruity Frosts

You will need:
   375 g (12 oz) white chocolate
   60 g (2 oz) Copha
   1 cup chopped dried apricots
   ½ cup toasted flaked almonds
   ½ cup coconut
   100 g (3½ oz) packet Chinese fried noodles

Melt white chocolate and Copha in a double saucepan over simmering heat. Stir in all other ingredients until well mixed. Spoon into paper patties and refrigerate until set. Store in an airtight container. Makes 30. *Plate 1*

French Chocolates

Very rich chocolate balls coated in crushed nuts or coconut—just perfect with after-dinner coffee!

You will need:
   375 g (12 oz) chocolate
   1 cup ground walnuts
   ¾ cup sweetened condensed milk
   1 teaspoon vanilla
   dash salt
   shredded coconut or chopped nuts

Melt chocolate in a double saucepan over simmering water. If you are unable to purchase ground walnuts, place whole walnuts in a plastic bag and crush with a rolling pin until very fine. Stir ground walnuts, sweetened condensed milk, vanilla and a dash of salt into chocolate. Allow to cool for five minutes. Roll into balls and coat with shredded coconut or chopped nuts. Refrigerate until set. Store in an airtight container. Makes 40. *Plate 3*

2. Cereal Treats

Cereal Treats are probably the easiest, most inexpensive, nourishing and popular treats you can make. The ingredients are always readily on hand, and the treats make good in-between snacks for children and adults alike. The recipes are so easy anyone can make them, and they aren't as sweet as some of the sugar-based treats.

Vary these recipes by substituting different cereals. When a new cereal comes out, think how you can incorporate it into some of the recipes for a pleasant change. The generic versions of the popular cereals are also suitable, with different flavourings and colourings dressing them up well.

It is worth keeping in mind that cereals can also be used for fillers in many savoury treats.

We've certainly come a long way with cereal recipes since the popular Chocolate Crackle first appeared, and no doubt there are many more recipes to come.

Honey Bubble Crunch

An easy treat to make which can be cut up and packaged in delicious honey-flavoured fingers.

You will need:
 ½ cup butter
 ½ cup sugar

 2 full tablespoons honey
 4 cups Rice Bubbles
 1 cup coconut

Chop butter into small pieces and combine butter, sugar and honey in a saucepan over low heat. Stir until brought to the boil and simmer for 3 to 4 minutes on low. Add Rice Bubbles and coconut. Stir quickly as mixture sets almost immediately. Press into a greased lamington tin and allow to set, about 5 to 10 minutes. Cut into squares or finger lengths. Makes 30 fingers.

Variations: Replace all or some of the Rice Bubbles with muesli, corn flakes, bran buds or nuts of any sort (chopped).

Suggested garnish: Drizzle melted chocolate in patterns over each finger to decorate. *Plate 5*

Weet-Bix Kids

Kids will love to make and eat these Weet-Bix-based balls which do not even need to be cooked.

You will need:
 9 Weet-Bix, crushed

1 cup coconut
1 tablespoon cocoa
1 cup mixed fruit
1 tin sweetened condensed milk
extra coconut for rolling

Mix dry ingredients. Pour over tin of sweetened condensed milk and blend well. Roll mixture into balls, and coat in coconut. Refrigerate to store. Makes 36. *Plate 5*

Oil muffin tins well and press thin layer of mixture over base and sides. Refrigerate until firm. To remove case, turn muffin tin over, hold hand underneath and press middle of shape hard—the cereal case will pop out in your hand. Alternatively, stand tin in warm water for a few seconds and gently ease case out with a thin knife. Fill with marshmallow or other filling of your choice, and garnish with cherries, strawberries, grated chocolate, and so on. (See recipe for marshmallow on page 35.) Makes 8 large muffin tin size. *Plate 6*

Cereal Cases

A special occasion chocolate-flavoured 'nest' to hold all kinds of delectable fillings.

You will need:
    120 g (4 oz) dark chocolate
    30 g (1 oz) Copha
    3 cups Rice Bubbles

Chop chocolate and Copha. Melt together over hot water in a double boiler. Slightly crush Rice Bubbles and pour melted chocolate mixture over.

Chocolate Roughs

A mouthwatering combination coated in chocolate goes wonderfully well with after-dinner coffee.

You will need:
    250 g (8 oz) butter
    1⅔ cups icing sugar
    ¾ cup rolled oats (uncooked)
    ¾ cup coconut
    ½ teaspoon coffee powder
    185 g (6 oz) cooking chocolate
    30 g (1 oz) Copha
    flavouring: vanilla, rum, brandy, or peppermint

Soften butter and cream butter and icing sugar. Work in rolled oats, coconut and coffee powder. Drop by teaspoonfuls onto greaseproof paper. Refrigerate and allow to harden for 30–40 minutes. Melt chopped cooking chocolate and Copha in a double boiler over simmering heat. Add flavouring. Using a fork, immerse each sweet into chocolate, lift out and place on waxed paper. Store in the refrigerator as after-dinner mints. Makes 30–36. *Plate 6*

Chocolate Roughs

Cherry Coconut Bars

Cherry Coconut Bars

Cherries and coconut make for a traditional flavour.

You will need:
  1 tin sweetened condensed milk
  125 g (4 oz) Copha
  1 tablespoon raspberry cordial
  2 cups bran buds
  125 g (4 oz) chopped glace cherries
  2 cups coconut

Topping
  200 g (6½ oz) cooking chocolate
  60 g (2 oz) Copha

Stir chopped Copha with sweetened condensed milk over low heat until melted. Cool slightly and add raspberry cordial, stirring until colour is even. Blend bran buds, chopped glace cherries and coconut in a bowl. Pour over condensed milk mixture. Press into a greaseproof paper-lined slice tin and refrigerate for 2 hours. Melt cooking chocolate and Copha in a double boiler over simmering water. Spread chocolate mixture over slice. Cool and store in refrigerator. Cut into bars or diamond shapes with a knife dipped in hot water. Makes 36. *Plate 6*

Bubbly Marshmallows

A rocky road type recipe which can have a delicious marshmallow and coconut topping.

You will need:
  3 heaped tablespoons cocoa
  250 g (8 oz) icing sugar
  4 cups Rice Bubbles
  250 g (8 oz) Copha
  125 g (4 oz) white or pink marshmallows

Topping (optional):
  125 g (4 oz) marshmallows
  coconut

Mix cocoa, icing sugar and Rice Bubbles together in a large bowl. Melt Copha over gentle heat and pour over dry ingredients. Add marshmallows and mix thoroughly. Press into a square tin, and refrigerate to set. Cut into squares. Makes 25.

To make topping, melt marshmallows in a double boiler over gently boiling water. Spread quickly over marshmallow mixture, and sprinkle with coconut before cutting into squares. *Plate 6*

Pink Mallow Bars

Truly delicious marshmallow bars which are so easy to make!

You will need:
  100 g (3½ oz) butter
  ½ cup castor sugar
  ½ teaspoon vanilla
  250 g (8 oz) pink marshmallows, chopped
  4 cups Rice Bubbles
  ½ cup crushed nuts
  100 g (3½ oz) dark chocolate chips

Melt butter in a pan, then add sugar, stirring until dissolved. Add vanilla and marshmallows, stirring until melted. Remove from heat. Add Rice Bubbles and nuts, mixing well.

Press mixture into greased lamington tin and allow to set. Melt chocolate chips and drizzle over Rice Bubble mixture. Allow to set before cutting into bars. Makes 18 large or 24 small. *Plate 5*

Honey Joys

An old favourite, always popular.

You will need:
  125 g (4 oz) butter
  ½ cup castor sugar
  2 tablespoons honey
  4 cups corn flakes (or Rice Bubbles)
  paper patty cases

Combine butter, sugar and honey in a saucepan, stirring over low heat until butter and sugar have melted. Allow to boil for 2–3 minutes. Remove from heat, stir in corn flakes, and then spoon mixture into paper cases sitting in patty tins. Allow to set. Makes 30. *Plate 7*

Note: If using Rice Bubbles, press into a lamington tin and leave for 10 minutes before cutting into fingers.

Variation: Add 1 cup of coconut to the cereal mixture, stirring in quickly as the mixture sets immediately.

3. Favourite Treats

The old-fashioned favourites such as butterscotch, barley sugar, toffee, popcorn and coconut ice are always popular and best sellers. This chapter gives some useful tips and guides for cooking toffees and popcorn, with some interesting variations, which will cost you next to nothing to make.

Toffee

We could write a book on toffees alone! Toffee is a cheap, easy sweet to make for fetes or any time. Children love toffees, and so do adults. You can include children in the making of toffees at the decorating stage. Be careful to keep the very hot liquid out of reach.

Sugar must be dissolved at a low temperature before boiling the mixture. Keep brushing down the sides of the pan with a brush dipped in warm water at this stage to keep crystals from forming and spoiling the toffee. Do not stir toffee once it has come to the boil unless specified in the recipe. Where milk is included in the recipe, cook at a lower temperature than water toffees. Plunge the pan of cooked toffee into a sink of cold water to quickly cool to working consistency. Then work quickly before it thickens too much.

Although sweet making is a great way to entertain children on rainy days, choose a dry, preferably cool day for fete cooking where you need the best results. Use the scrapings on the bottom of the pan from toffees for home treats, as the quality of this part of the toffee differs from the free flowing top portion.

Toffee Testing

Thread   106–113°C (223–236°F): Drop a small amount of hot toffee into a bowl of iced water. If it forms a fine thin thread, it is at the thread stage.

Soft Ball   112–116°C (234–240°F): A small amount dropped into a bowl of iced water will form a soft sticky ball when held between your fingers that will flatten but not disintegrate.

Hard Ball   121–130°C (250–266°F): A small amount dropped into a bowl of iced water will feel firm and hold its shape when rolled between the fingers.

Hard Crack   149–154°C (300–310°F): A small amount dropped into a bowl of iced water will not be sticky when removed, will snap easily, and have a golden colour.

A marble slab is great for making toffees as it is cool and absorbs heat quickly and evenly. If you do not have a marble slab, use a sheet of non-stick baking paper on the work bench.

Use your imagination in making toffees. The list of varieties you can come up with is endless. Although the old favourites always sell well at fetes, people are naturally curious and will be eager to taste any new sensations you can think of. Vary the colours, add ingredients such as nuts, sprinkles, coconut, popcorn, cereals and health

Butterscotch

foods (sesame seeds, poppy seeds, sunflower seeds, pine nuts and so on) and make alternative shapes such as umbrellas, lollypops, twists and rounds.

Toffees can be presented wrapped, boxed, in patty papers, packaged in glass jars, tins, glasses, cellophane paper or bags, boxes, cardboard or cane baskets.

Experiment with different syrups. Instead of honey, use treacle, molasses or maple syrup. Try different types of honey, such as light blended honeys, dark honeys, iron bark, stringy bark or Patterson's Curse honeys (famous varieties of Mudgee honeys are especially good).

Try using milk or sweetened condensed milk or butter in toffees for a creamier taste. Experiment between fetes, making small batches, perhaps trying one variation a month, and share your discoveries with others.

Butterscotch

Old-fashioned butterscotch with a creamy consistency.

You will need:
   3 cups sugar
   ¾ cup butter
   1 cup boiling water
   ½ teaspoon vanilla essence

Combine butter, sugar and water and stir until sugar has dissolved and mixture is boiling. Boil without stirring until brittle when tested in iced water. (It takes about 45 minutes to reach this stage.) Add vanilla and pour into a greased 20 cm square tin. When nearly set mark into small squares with a buttered knife. Sprinkle with chopped nuts if desired to garnish. Makes 36 small squares. *Plate 9*

Barley Sugar

This mixture cooks and hardens quickly, so work fast to twist it into strips.

You will need:
   2 cups white sugar
   1¼ cups water
   pinch cream of tartar
   rind 1 lemon, thinly peeled

In a heavy pan stir white sugar and water over moderate heat until sugar is dissolved. (If crystals form on sides of pan, brush down with a brush dipped in warm water. Add cream of tartar and lemon rind. Bring to the boil without stirring. Boil gently without stirring until hard crack stage. Remove from heat and discard lemon rind. Pour mixture onto non-stick baking paper, and leave to cool for a few minutes.

Oil some scissors and use to cut mixture into strips while still on the paper. Peel paper off each strip and twist gently but quickly while mixture is still warm. You can also twist into cane or knot shapes (use your imagination). Store in an airtight container. Makes approximately 1. strips or 40 pieces. *Plate 9*

Umbrella Toffees and School Toffees

You will need:
   3 cups sugar
   1 cup water
   ¼ cup brown vinegar
   coconut, 100s and 1000s, chopped nuts for garnish
   small wooden sticks

Combine sugar, water and brown vinegar in a large pan. Stir over low heat until sugar has dissolved. Increase heat and boil rapidly for approximately 15 minutes. Test for hard crack stage in iced water. Remove from heat and

Plate 1 (clockwise from top): Fruity Frosts (p.13), Chocolate Spiders (p.13), Chocolate Prunes with Port (p.12), Apricot Ambrosia (p.13) and Easy Home-made Chocolates (p.12)

CHOCOLATE TREATS

Plate 2: Chocolate Cherries (p.11)

Plate 3: French Chocolates coated in chopped nuts, sprinkles and coconut (p.14)

Plate 4: Chocolate Ginger (p.12)

Plate 5 (left to right): Honey Bubble Crunch (p.15) under dome, Pink Mallow Bars (p.17) and Weet-Bix Kids (p.15)

CEREAL TREATS

Plate 6 (clockwise from top): Chocolate Roughs (p.16), Bubby Marshmallows (p.17) in bowl, Cereal Cases filled with marshmallow (p.16) and Cherry Coconut Bars (p.17)

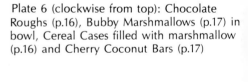

Plate 7: Honey Joys (p.18)

22

8

Plate 8 (clockwise from top): Candy Popcorn (p.26), Umbrella Toffees and School Toffees (p.20), Sherbet Bags (p.27) and Chocolate Crackles (p.27)

FAVOURITE TREATS

Plate 9 (clockwise from left): Butterscotch (p.20), Candy Popcorn (p.26), Barley Sugar (p.20), Toffee Apples (p.25), Caramel Popcorn (p.26) and Coconut Ice (p.26)

9

Plate 10: Apricot Surprises
(p.28) and Marzipan Log (p.29)

Plate 11: Moonshine Biffs (p.28)
and Peanut Butter Balls (p.29)

Plate 12: Pine Nut Toffee (p.30),
Easy Rocky Road (p.28), Sesame
Caramel Toffee (p.30) and Sesame
Snaps (p.30) in foreground

...llow bubbles to subside. Pour into well greased patty ...ins and decorate tops with suggested garnishes. Push a ...wooden stick into the middle of each toffee and decorate ...vith gift ribbon with curled ends. This mixture makes 36 ...Jmbrella Toffees, and if poured into paper patty cases ...vill make 36 School Toffees. *Plate 8*

Toffee Apples

You will need:

  8 small red apples
  8 wooden skewers
  3 cups sugar
  ½ cup glucose
  ½ cup water
  1 teaspoon red food colouring
  vanilla

...Wash and dry apples and remove stems. Push skewers ...nto stem ends of apples.

  Combine sugar, glucose and water in deep saucepan. ...ook over medium heat, stirring constantly, until mixture ...oils. Then cook without stirring until small amount ...ested in iced water is at hard ball stage. Remove from ...eat, add flavouring and colouring, stirring only to mix. ...old each apple by skewer end and quickly twirl in

syrup, tilting saucepan to cover. Allow excess to drip off, then stand on lightly greased trays to cool. Makes 8. *Plate 9*

  If you are unable to obtain wooden skewers, use four thin satay sticks with pointed ends trimmed off. Bind the sticks together by winding gift ribbon around, securing and curling ribbon ends to decorate.

Popcorn

Children love to make popcorn—and if you have a large saucepan with a glass lid it is great fun to gather the kids around and watch the popcorn popping. This causes many laughs and is great entertainment on rainy days.

  Use your imagination with popcorn. You can flavour it with herbs, chicken/onion/garlic salts, cheeses and chilli mixtures. You can combine it with other savouries such as nuts, pretzels, chips and flavoured cereals.

  For sweet popcorn, you can simply sprinkle it with butter and icing sugar, coat it with toffee or candies, or add coconut, colourings, sprinkles and so on. Experiment—it is cheap and good fun!

Basic Recipe

Cover the base of a large saucepan (preferably one with a glass lid) with 2 tablespoons of oil (experiment with different oils), melted butter or margarine. To test, throw two kernels of popping corn into the saucepan and cover with the lid. When these kernels pop, the oil is just right for you to add ½ cup of corn. Cover with lid, and gently shake the pan to keep the unpopped kernels on the bottom of the saucepan close to the heat. Keep the heat low at this stage so as not to burn the popcorn. Keep shaking, gently, and *do not remove the lid* until the popping has *stopped*! Immediately remove from heat and flavour according to your taste and imagination. Delicious eaten hot or cold. Store in an airtight container. Makes about 5 cups of popped corn.

Candy Popcorn

Popcorn is so cheap and easy to make, and coloured popcorn is especially appealing to children.

You will need:
  ½ cup popping corn
  2 tablespoons oil
  2 cups sugar
  1 cup water
  ½ teaspoon food colouring

Heat oil in a large saucepan until very hot. Test with a few kernels of corn until they have popped, add rest of corn and cover the pan, shaking constantly over medium heat until popping ceases. Remove from heat, turn out of pan and allow to cool.

Caramel Popcorn

Place sugar, water and food colouring in pan, stirring over low heat until all sugar is dissolved. Bring to boil, and boil rapidly until toffee is at hard crack stage when tested in cold water. Remove from heat and pour over popcorn. Stir toffee constantly through popcorn until it is all well coated. Turn out onto trays to cool. Store in airtight bags or containers. Makes approximately 5 cups. *Plate 8*

Make fresh batches of popcorn for different colours, and then layer in jars or bags for added effect, or mix all the colours together for a very colourful result.

Caramel Popcorn

A delicious caramel-flavoured popcorn with the added taste of peanuts.

You will need:
  ½ cup popping corn
  2 tablespoons oil
  125 g (4 oz) butter
  2 tablespoons honey
  ¾ cup sugar
  ½ cup peanuts

Heat oil in large saucepan. Add corn and cover, shaking saucepan constantly until popping ceases. Remove popcorn from heat.

Mix honey, sugar and butter in a saucepan, stirring over low heat until sugar is dissolved. Bring to boil, and boil uncovered for 5 minutes.

Remove from heat, add peanuts to syrup, and pour over popcorn. Mix until popcorn is well coated. Spread onto greased baking trays to cool. Break into approximately 10–15 large pieces and package in airtight containers, cellophane or plastic bags. *Plate 9*

Coconut Ice

Coconut Ice is a long time favourite with everyone, and a best seller.

You will need:
  500 g (16 oz) icing sugar
  250 g (8 oz) coconut
  1 teaspoon vanilla
  2 egg whites
  125 g (4 oz) Copha
  food colouring

Mix icing sugar, coconut and vanilla in a bowl. Beat egg whites lightly and mix in. Melt Copha, cool slightly, and then pour over mixture in bowl, stirring well. Divide mixture in half. Press one half into a greased 20 cm square tin. Mix food colouring into other half, and press this coloured mixture firmly on top. Chill in refrigerator and then cut into small bars. Makes 18 bars or 25 squares. *Plate 9*

Chocolate Crackles

Ever-popular Chocolate Crackles are easy enough for the kids to make and decorate.

You will need:
  250 g (8 oz) Copha, melted
  4 cups Rice Bubbles
  1 cup icing sugar
  ¼ cup cocoa
  1 cup coconut

Combine all ingredients thoroughly. Spoon into coloured patty cases and decorate with 100s and 1000s, Smarties and other sweets. Makes 45 medium Chocolate Crackles. Keep refrigerated. *Plate 8*

Sherbet

Sherbet brings back old time memories of childhood—and it's cheap and easy to make!

You will need:
  700 g (23 oz) pure icing sugar
  225 g (7 oz) bicarbonate of soda
  200 g (6½ oz) citric acid powder
  3 or 4 drops oil of lemon or lemon essence

Put each of the icing sugar, bicarbonate of soda and citric acid powder separately in the oven to dry at 100–110°C (212–230°F) for 10 minutes. Mix together and add oil of lemon or lemon essence. Put through a fine sieve three times, and store in an airtight container. Makes approximately 4 cups. Measure into small bags with a dessertspoon.

For fetes, place a teaspoonful in small cones with marshmallow on top (see recipes for Marshmallow on page 35), or in small bags with tops folded in from corner and a small straw or liquorice stick inserted to lick the sherbet. *Plate 8*

Honeycomb

Choose a dry day to make this golden honeycomb.

You will need:
  2 tablespoons golden syrup
  2 tablespoons honey
  ¾ cup sugar
  2 tablespoons water
  1½ teaspoons bicarbonate of soda

Place golden syrup, honey, sugar and water in a large saucepan. Cook until honeycomb sets hard in a cup of iced water. Take off heat. Add bicarbonate of soda. Beat the mixture and it will rise and increase in bulk considerably. Pour into a well greased large tray as it falls, without spreading or patting the mixture. When cold and set, cut or break into pieces. Makes 10–15 large pieces.

4. Sweet Treats

Explore a mouthwatering selection of different types of treats suitable for gift giving or for sale (when packaged attractively) in this Sweet Treats section.

Moonshine Biffs

Melt-in-the-mouth Moonshine Biffs are everyone's favourite.

You will need:
    3 dessertspoons gelatine
    250 g (8 oz) sugar
    1¼ cups water
    250 g (8 oz) icing sugar
    1 teaspoon vanilla essence
    coconut or icing sugar

Place gelatine, sugar and water in a pan. Boil for 8 minutes and allow to cool. Add icing sugar and vanilla essence. Beat with an electric mixer until thick and white. Wet an oblong tin and pour mixture in. Leave for 24 hours. Cut into squares using a wet knife to prevent ragged edges. Roll in coconut or icing sugar. Makes 24 large or 40 small squares. Best refrigerated in an airtight container until ready for use or sale. *Plate 11*

Easy Rocky Road

A combination of yummy ingredients which is so eas[y] to make.

You will need:
    3 heaped tablespoons cocoa
    250 g (8 oz) icing sugar
    4 cups Rice Bubbles
    250 g (8 oz) Copha
    150 g (5 oz) pink and white marshmallows
    peanuts and glace cherries (optional)

Sift cocoa and icing sugar together. Place in bowl wit[h] Rice Bubbles. Melt Copha over gentle heat until warm[,] not hot. Add to dry ingredients. Snip marshmallows int[o] small pieces, add to mixture and stir thoroughly. (You ma[y] wish to add peanuts and glace cherries at this point.) Pres[s] into a lightly greased oblong tin. Place in refrigerator t[o] set and then cut into pieces. Makes 48. *Plate 12*

Apricot Surprises

Dried apricots stuffed with marzipan soaked in port w[ill] be a delightful surprise—a great idea for gift giving.

Chop marzipan into small pieces in a bowl. Knead in mixed dried fruit and rum, brandy or port to flavour, until well blended. Use icing sugar to prevent sticking. Shape into log and dust with icing sugar. Refrigerate until firm and then cut into thin slices. Store in layers in an airtight container with waxed paper. For presentation, arrange slices on a plate or in a box, and cover to make airtight. Makes 60. *Plate 10*

Peanut Butter Balls

Delicious peanut-flavoured balls coated with coconut.

You will need:

ou will need:
200 g (6½ oz) dried apricots
4 tablespoons port or marsala
100 g (3½ oz) marzipan
sifted icing sugar

oak dried apricots in port or marsala for 4–5 hours. rain, reserving liquid, then dry on kitchen paper. Knead eserved liquid into marzipan with just enough icing ugar to prevent sticking. Roll marzipan into small balls. it each apricot and stuff each with a marzipan ball, then atten out. Store between sheets of waxed paper in rtight containers in refrigerator until ready to package o on a plate or shallow box to give or sell. Makes about 5–30. *Plate 10*

Marzipan Log

Marzipan Log can be cut into colourful slices for resentation.

ou will need:
250 g (8 oz) marzipan
375 g (12 oz) mixed dried fruit with imitation cherries
4 tablespoons rum, brandy or port
icing sugar

You will need:
½ cup peanut butter
½ cup milk
1½ cups brown sugar
1 tablespoon golden syrup
15 g (½ oz) butter
1 teaspoon vanilla
coconut or wheatgerm

In a heavy saucepan, stir peanut butter, milk, brown sugar and golden syrup over low heat with a wooden spoon until sugar is dissolved. Then bring to the boil and boil gently until soft ball stage is reached (page 19). Remove from heat. Add butter and vanilla, stir through to mix and let cool. When cool enough to handle, roll into balls and toss in coconut or wheatgerm to coat. Store in refrigerator. Makes 30. *Plate 11*

29

Sesame Caramel Toffee

The distinctive taste of sesame seeds makes this toffee especially good.

You will need:
   1 cup castor sugar
   90 g (3 oz) butter
   ½ cup sweetened condensed milk
   ⅓ cup glucose syrup
   2 tablespoons golden syrup
   1 cup sesame seeds, toasted (available in bulk from
      health food shops)

Cook castor sugar, butter, sweetened condensed milk, glucose and golden syrup over low heat, without boiling, until sugar is dissolved. Brush sides of saucepan with brush dipped in warm water to prevent crystallisation. Stirring constantly, bring to the boil and boil uncovered, continuing to stir, for approximately 15 minutes to hard ball stage (page 19). Stir in sesame seeds. Spread into a greased 20 cm square tin. Cool for 15 minutes and turn out of tin. Cut into finger lengths while still warm. Wrap in cellophane. Makes 20. *Plate 12*

Pine Nut Toffees

The unusual dark toffee with the flavour of pine nuts will be relished by men in particular.

You will need:
   2 cups white sugar
   ½ cup water
   pinch cream of tartar
   2 teaspoons plain flour
   1 tablespoon cocoa
   400 g (13 oz) pine nuts or unsalted peanuts

In a heavy saucepan, cook sugar and water ove moderate heat until sugar is dissolved. Brush sides c saucepan with brush dipped in warm water to preven crystallisation. Add cream of tartar and boil to soft ba stage (page 19). Remove from heat. Stir in flour, coco and pine nuts. Turn out onto oiled marble slab or bakin sheet. Flatten out, and when cold break into pieces. Wra in cellophane or small plastic bags tied with gift ribbon Makes 8–10 large pieces. *Plate 12*

Sesame Snaps

'Open Sesame' . . . Ali Baba would have enjoyed thi Arabian toffee in ancient times—it's unusual and tast

You will need:
   1 cup white sugar
   1 cup sesame seeds (available in bulk from health
      food shops)

In a heavy saucepan cook both ingredients over low hea stirring constantly. After about ten minutes the sugar wi be melted and mixture will be golden. Pour onto an oile baking sheet and spread. Cut into bars while still warr or break into pieces when cold. Wrap in waxed pape plastic wrap or cellophane bonbon style and store in a airtight jar. Makes 10. *Plate 12*

5. Kids' Treats

Packaging Ideas

Kids will enjoy making many of the easy treats in this chapter, which are not only fun to make and decorate, but yummy too! There are lots of different ways to present sweets for children, whether for a birthday party or for sale on the candy stall at the school fete. Inexpensive crepe paper, cellophane and gift paper can be fashioned into a number of different containers for sweets.

Umbrellas

Cut colourful crepe paper into 20–25 cm (8″–10″) circles (use a dinner plate as a pattern). Fold and cut in half to make two semicircles. Form semicircle into a cone shape and stitch straight sides together to make a cone. Half fill cone with lollies and place a candy cane or a chenille stick in the middle for an umbrella handle. To decorate, tie around the middle with gift ribbon.

UMBRELLA

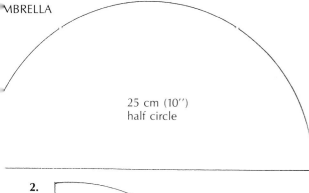

25 cm (10″)
half circle

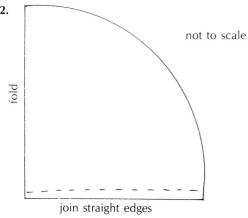

2.

not to scale

fold

join straight edges

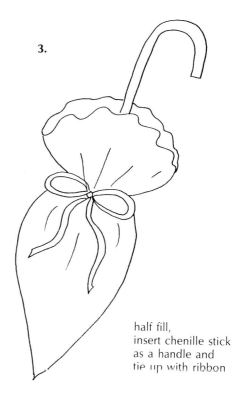

3.

half fill,
insert chenille stick
as a handle and
tie up with ribbon

Carrots

Orange and green crepe paper make terrific 'carrots' for lollies, and are especially good for popcorn. Cut a 25 cm (10″) circle of orange crepe paper in half to form two semicircles. Cut a strip of green crepe paper 40 cm (16″) long and 10–15 cm (4″–6″) wide. Cut 5–7 cm (2″–3″) slits along one 40 cm (16″) side to make carrot tops. Glue or sew carrot tops to curved edge of orange semicircle. Form semicircle into a cone shape and join straight edges. Half fill with popcorn or other candy and tie with gift ribbon between orange body and carrot tops to form plump carrots (see next page).

Flowers

Place a handful of sweets or popcorn in a 20 cm (8″) square of coloured cellophane or crepe paper. Secure

31

CARROT

1.

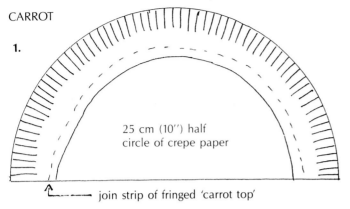

25 cm (10″) half circle of crepe paper

↑
└─── join strip of fringed 'carrot top'

2.

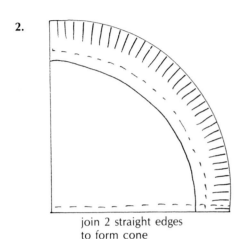

join 2 straight edges to form cone

3.

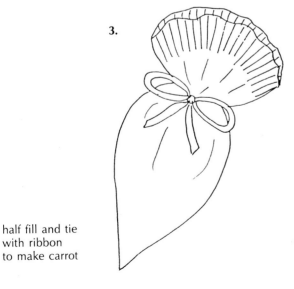

half fill and tie with ribbon to make carrot

FLOWER

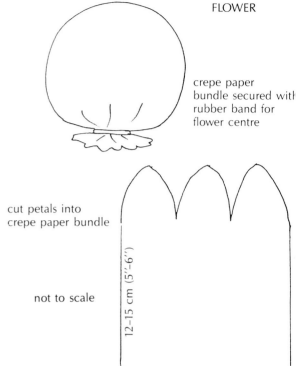

crepe paper bundle secured with rubber band for flower centre

cut petals into crepe paper bundle

12–15 cm (5″–6″)

not to scale

bundle with rubber band. Cut a pack of crepe paper into widths of 12–15 cm (5″–6″) . Cut 2 or 3 petal shapes into one edge of crepe paper. Unwind approximately 50–60 cm (20″–25″) of petals and wind around cellophane or crepe paper bundle to form petals as for a flower. Secure crepe paper to cellophane bundle with another small rubber band and trim any excess.

Gift Paper Bags

You can make your own super little gift paper bags in different sizes. The following is a good size for sweets. Cut colourful gift paper into 24 × 15 cm (10″ × 6″) pieces. Fold top 24 cm (10″) edge under once and glue in place. Fold each side into the middle to form an overlapping centre back seam. Glue this overlapped edge. Fold up bottom edge of bag 1 cm at the back and glue in position. Punch two holes in the top edge of each side of bag with a hole punch. Thread both ends of 25 cm (10″) length of ribbon, thick wool or cord through the four holes and knot the two ends together to form a carry handle.

Bonbons

Colourful gift paper, crepe paper or cellophane can be used to make simple bonbons. You need a cardboard cylinder approximately 10–12 cm (4″–5″) long, or make your own from light cardboard secured with sticky tape.

GIFT PAPER BAGS

1.

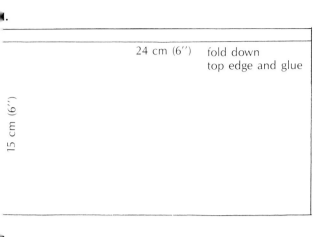

24 cm (6″)   fold down
top edge and glue

15 cm (6″)

2.

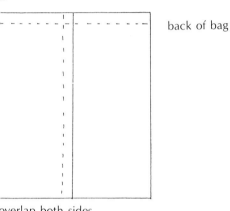

back of bag

overlap both sides
to form a back 'seam'
and glue

3.

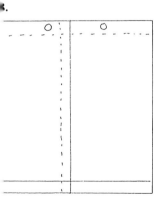

punch 4 holes in
top edge for
carry handle

fold up
bottom edge
and glue

Cut paper or cellophane twice the length of the cylinder. With the cylinder in the middle, secure with sticky tape. Use gift ribbon to tie up one end of the bonbon. Insert Iollies or small sweets into the bonbon and then tie up open end. Bonbons can be decorated with cut-out motifs, the ends can be fringed, and they make wonderful surprise decorations for a Christmas tree. See examples in Plate 34.

Cardboard Baskets

A square shape of any size is easy to cut out and assemble into a basket using coloured cardboard and a stapler. Varying the height of the sides of the basket makes different shaped baskets from the same size pattern. Children might like to decorate the sides of the basket with coloured Texta pens.

A good size for presenting sweets is 18 cm square with 3 cm sides for a shallow basket or 4 cm sides for a deeper basket. Cut in four places as shown in the diagram. Fold along dotted lines, tuck each corner in behind each side and staple in position. Cut a strip of cardboard of a suitable length, 1–2 cm wide, and staple in place on either side of the basket to form a handle. See examples in Plates 32, 33 and 34.

1.

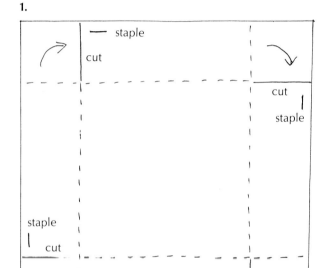

staple
cut

cut
staple

staple
cut

staple

cut

Not to scale: Sweet basket 18 cm square with 3–4 cm sides. Cut where shown. Fold on dotted lines, to form sides, tucking corners inside basket and stapling where indicated.

2.

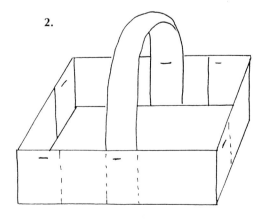

33

Truccles

Yummy chocolate balls the kids can easily make and roll in coconut.

You will need:
   1 cup coconut
   250 g (8 oz) sweet biscuits, crushed
   400 g (1¼ cups) sweetened condensed milk
   250 g (8 oz) icing sugar (1 cup)
   1½ tablespoons cocoa
   extra coconut for coating

Combine all ingredients except extra coconut in a bowl until well mixed. Take teaspoonfuls of mixture and make into small balls and roll in coconut. Makes 50–60. *Plate 14*

Note: Use Honey Snap, Ginger Nut or oatmeal biscuits for different flavourings.

Strawberries

These delicious sweets look and taste just like real strawberries!

You will need:
   ½ cup milk
   ¼ cup sugar
   1 cup coconut
   1 packet strawberry jelly crystals
   1 cup ground almonds
   ¼ teaspoon almond essence
   Mint Leaves sweets for garnish (optional)

Mix milk and sugar together in a saucepan, stirring over low heat until sugar is dissolved. Combine milk mix with remaining ingredients in bowl and refrigerate until firm enough to handle. Pull off small pieces and roll into strawberry-sized balls. Decorate with Mint Leaves fo strawberry leaves if desired. Store in refrigerator. Presen in small patty cases or in a basket or box lined with shredded cellophane. Makes 24. *Plate 15*

Edible Animals

Cute Edible Animals will be irresistible to children.

You will need:
   1 packet cake mix
   icing sugar, food colouring or cocoa
   jubes, chocolate bullets, silver cachous, slivered
      almonds and marshmallows to decorate

Make up cake mix as directed on packet. Drop heaped teaspoonfuls into patty papers. Bake in a moderate over for 12 to 15 minutes. Cool on a wire rack. Makes 24 *Plate 14*

Decorate Edible Animals as follows:

Echidna
Cover cake shape in chocolate icing made with cocoa Insert chocolate bullet at one end for a long nose, and position two silver cachous for eyes. Insert slivere almonds all over body at an angle for spines.

Turned Turtle
Cover cake shape with icing coloured with green foo colouring. Press in a round jube at one end for a head Insert four chocolate bullets for legs to make a turtl turned on its back.

Rabbit

Cover cake shape with white icing. Cut a pink marshmallow into long pieces, and press two pieces in position as ears. Cut up a pink jube into small pieces and insert two as pink eyes. Press a round pink jube in place as a tail. Use a silver cachou for the nose. *Plate 14*

Marzipan Animals and Shapes

Colourful marzipan animals and shapes just waiting to be eaten!

You will need:
    200 g (6½ oz) marzipan
    food colourings
    cookie cutters in various shapes

Knead marzipan on a marble slab or tray until pliable. Divide into sections and add separate food colourings, and again knead until mixture is supple and can be rolled out to a 1 cm thickness. Use animal and other cookie cutter shapes and decorate with bows, tails, etc. Makes 20 to 30 shapes depending on size. *Plate 15*

Marshmallow

Easy and versatile Marshmallow can be used in lots of different ways.

Basic Recipe

You will need:
    1¼ cups castor sugar
    1 tablespoon gelatine
    1 cup boiling water

Stir gelatine into boiling water, tip onto sugar and beat until thick with electric mixer.

Marshmallow Cones
    Basic marshmallow recipe
    flat-bottomed icecream cones
    sprinkles, Smarties, etc.
    Sherbet (optional—see recipe on page 27)

Make up basic recipe for marshmallow. Spoon into icecream cones and decorate with sprinkles, Smarties, and so on. You may wish to add a teaspoon of Sherbet in the bottom of each cone.

Marshmallow Cups
    basic marshmallow recipe
    food colourings
    plastic wine glasses or plastic cups
    100s and 1000s

Make up basic recipe for marshmallow. Divide mixture into three bowls, add a few drops of different food colouring to each bowl and mix in thoroughly. Spoon layers of different coloured marshmallow into plastic cups or glasses. Cover with plastic wrap, and tie on a plastic spoon with gift ribbon. *Plate 13*

Marshmallow Cones

Marshmallow Cups

Smartie Squares

So many colourful goodies in Smartie Squares, which is why they are so popular.

You will need:
    1½ cups coconut
    1½ cups self raising flour
    ½ cup brown sugar
    125 g (4 oz) margarine

Mix all dry ingredients together. Pour on melted margarine and mix well. Press into a lamington tin. Bake at 170°C (335°F) in a fan-forced oven or at 180°C (350°F) in a regular oven for 15 minutes. Allow to cool.

Topping
    basic marshmallow recipe (page 35)
    chopped marshmallows, chocolate chips, Smarties,
        sprinkles, etc.

Spread marshmallow mixture over base, and sprinkle suggested toppings evenly over the marshmallow. Allow to set and cut into squares. Makes 24 squares or 16 large rectangles. *Plate 13*

Funny Faces

The kids will really enjoy turning simple biscuits into Funny Faces with just some marshmallow and a few colourful sweets.

You will need:
    packet of plain sweet round or oval shaped biscuits
    Smarties and sprinkles
    basic marshmallow mix (page 35)

Spread marshmallow on tops of biscuits. Work quickly to make faces with Smarties for eyes, nose and mouth and sprinkles for hair before marshmallow sets. Makes 24 or more. *Plate 13*

Gingerbread Men

Kids just love Gingerbread Men, especially if they can be involved in decorating them too! This recipe makes up a large quantity of gingerbread shapes, depending on how thinly you roll out the dough, and how big your cutters are. They are also great sellers.

You will need:
    ½ cup butter or margarine, softened
    ½ cup brown sugar
    ½ cup treacle
    2½ cups plain flour
    1 cup self raising flour
    1 teaspoon cinnamon
    1 teaspoon ginger
    ½ teaspoon salt
    ¼ teaspoon ground cloves
    ⅓ cup water

Cream butter and sugar and beat in treacle. Mix dry ingredients together and blend in, adding alternately with water. Work dough until smooth. Roll out and cut out required shapes. Bake in 180°C (350°F) oven for 8–10 minutes. Makes approximately 20 large Gingerbread Men or several dozen small shapes. *Plate 15*

Plate 13 (clockwise from left): Crepe paper flowers and carrots (p.31), Marshmallow Cones and Marshmallow Cups (p.35), crepe paper umbrellas (p.31), Funny Faces (p.36) and Smartie Squares (p.36)

KIDS' TREATS

Plate 14: Edible Animals (p.34) and Truccles (p.34)

Plate 15: Strawberries (p.34), Gingerbread Men (p.36) and Marzipan Animals and Shapes (p.35)

Plate 16 (left to right): Muesli Munchies (p.43), Apricot Rounds (p.41) and Date Slice (p.42)

Plate 17: Candied Peel (p.43)

SNACK TREATS

Plate 18 (left to right): Carrot Candies (p.41), Peanut Butter Squares (p.43) and Muesli Bars (p.42) in jar

Plate 19 (clockwise from top): Pizza Popcorn (p.46), Chilli Nuts (p.46) and Curried Nuts and Bolts (p.45)

Plate 20 (left to right): Herb Twists (p.46), Cheese Rounds (p.45) and Caraway Sticks (p.44) with Devilled Raisins (p.45) in foreground

Plate 21 (left to right): Coffee Pecans (p.50), Creamy Peanut Balls (p.49) and Sugar Coated Peanuts (p.49)

NUTTY TREATS

Plate 22 (left to right): Nutty Honey Chews (p.48), Orange Sugared Pecans (p.48) and Ginger Peanut Toffee (p.49)

6. Snack Treats

Snack Treats are wonderful to have on hand for play-lunches, picnics and in-between meals snacks. Although not strictly 'health food', they are an opportunity to feed the family some of the more unusual seeds, nuts and fruits that we may otherwise neglect.

Some people also do not like cereal and milk in its traditional form for breakfast, so cereals, milk powders, nuts and seeds combined together in various snack treats can be substituted. People who are 'too busy' for breakfast can substitute some of the snack treats. Even though such treats may contain sugar, they will have the rest of the day to burn off the energy.

Snack treats are very useful at sporting events. They provide quick, instant energy to burn and their high content of cereals, seeds and nuts provides fibre. They are also a good 'tide me over till I get home' treat to fill an empty tummy.

Packaged attractively, they will make great sellers at market days and fetes, and instant energy food for the family to take on outings.

Carrot Candies

Carrots would seem an unlikely ingredient for a candy, but these Carrot Candies are unusual and delicious.

You will need:
    1½ cups white sugar
    ¼ cup water
    500 g (16 oz) grated carrots
    1 teaspoon fresh ginger, grated
    ½ cup walnuts, chopped
    2 tablespoons lemon juice

In a heavy pan heat and stir white sugar and water until sugar is dissolved. Mix in carrots and lemon juice and bring to the boil. Boil for 30 minutes or until very thick. Remove from heat and stir in grated ginger and chopped walnuts. Pour into greased 15 cm square tin and allow to cool and set. Cut into squares and wrap in waxed paper or cellophane. Makes 36. *Plate 18*

Apricot Rounds

Apricots and coconut make these rounds especially tasty.

You will need:
    125 g (4 oz) dried apricots, chopped
    ½ cup water
    ⅓ cup chopped almonds
    1 teaspoon grated lemon rind
    1 teaspoon lemon juice
    1 teaspoon orange juice
    ½ cup honey
    1 cup skim milk powder
    1 tablespoon wheatgerm
    ½ cup sultanas
    ½ cup coconut
    coconut for coating

Simmer water, honey and chopped apricots for ten minutes or until apricots are tender. Do not drain. Add remaining ingredients except for coconut to be used for coating. Mix all ingredients well. Divide into three sections, and roll each section into a sausage shape 20 cm (8'') long. Roll in extra coconut to coat. Refrigerate for several hours before cutting into slices. Makes 55–60. *Plate 16*

Apricot Rounds (page 41)

Date Slices

Delightful Date Slices will be firm favourites.

You will need:
    250 g (8 oz) dates, chopped
    ½ cup sugar
    ½ cup coconut
    60 g (2 oz) butter
    1 tablespoon lemon juice
    1 teaspoon vanilla
    3 cups Rice Bubbles
    60 g (2 oz) peanuts

Combine butter, sugar and chopped dates in a saucepan, and stir over medium heat until dates are soft and pulpy, about five minutes. Remove from heat, beat until smooth, and then allow to stand for five minutes. Add remaining ingredients and mix well. Spread mixture evenly in 20 cm (8″) square tin which has been both greased and lined with greased paper. Refrigerate and set before cutting into slices. Makes 16. *Plate 16*

Note: Especially good topped with a lemon flavoured icing.

Muesli Bars

Ever popular Muesli Bars make great treats for lunchboxes, picnics or snacks.

You will need:
    2 cups toasted muesli
    1 cup coconut
    ½ cup sultanas (prunes, dates or dried apricots may be substituted)
    125 g (4 oz) butter or margarine
    ⅓ cup honey

Mix muesli, coconut and sultanas in a bowl. Melt butter and honey over a low heat. Add to the dry ingredients and stir well. Spread mixture in a greased and paper-lined 20 cm square slab tin. Chill until set. Cut into bars when set. Makes 12. *Plate 18*

Note: You may wish to top with drizzled chocolate or a lemon icing.

Candied Peel

Candied Peel

This is a good way to use up citrus fruit peels instead of throwing them away.

You will need:

    6 orange/lemon/grapefruit skins
    4 cups sugar
    2 cups water
    castor sugar

When peeling fruit include the white pith as it becomes clear when cooked and looks very attractive. Cut in strips.

Boil skins in water until tender. Drain, then boil again in fresh water for 20 minutes. Bring 4 cups of sugar and 2 cups of water to boil, stirring until sugar is dissolved. Add peel and boil until syrup has almost gone. Lower heat as liquid reduces and stir to prevent burning.

Remove peel, spread on waxed paper and leave to dry in the sun or in a very cool oven (50°C/120°F) for 30–45 minutes. Do not overdry.

Roll peel in castor sugar when dry. Store in airtight jars. Makes enough peel to fill a 2 litre jar. *Plate 17*

Muesli Munchies

A delightful blend of muesli, coconut, dried apricots and chocolate.

You will need:

    3 cups muesli
    ¼ cup icing sugar
    1 cup coconut
    1 cup dried apricots, chopped
    200 g (6½ oz) cooking chocolate, chopped
    50 g (1½ oz) Copha
    patty papers

Combine 3 cups of muesli, icing sugar, coconut and dried apricots in a large bowl. Melt chopped cooking chocolate and Copha in a double saucepan over hot water. Pour over muesli mixture and blend well. Work quickly to place spoonfuls in patty papers. Allow to set in refrigerator. Makes 40. *Plate 16*

Peanut Butter Squares

Peanut butter gives these squares their delicious flavour, and they are so quick and easy to make.

You will need:

    375 g (12 oz) peanut butter
    4 tablespoons honey
    4 tablespoons golden syrup
    3 teaspoons orange juice
    4 cups Rice Bubbles

Heat peanut butter, honey, golden syrup and orange juice over low heat for 2–3 minutes until well blended. Fold in Rice Bubbles and mix well. Press mixture into a greased lamington tin and refrigerate at least 2 hours until firm. Cut into squares to serve. Makes 30. *Plate 18*

7. Savoury Treats

Although a relatively new idea, savoury treats will be the foundation of a lot of new recipes. Be on the lookout for things to use as the base of your treat: popcorn, cereals, pastries, snack foods, nuts and commercial biscuits. Then look for combinations of spices, herbs, flavours, packet soups and casserole bases, for example, that can be used to create an interesting new treat!

Savoury Treats have special appeal to men. As many of the treats can be made up in bulk, they can be packaged up for Father's Day stalls. As some of the recipes are fairly simple, even children, with supervision, can have fun making nibblies for their dads.

Instead of spending money on expensive packaged goods, economical Savoury Treats will be great for the household budget too! As they can be stored in airtight containers, you can have a tasty treat on hand to serve to unexpected guests.

Savoury Treats, packaged up in boxes, bags, bundles or jars, tied with generous amounts of curled gift ribbon, make welcome gifts to a hostess as well as very acceptable gifts for Christmas or Father's Day.

You will need:
   3 sheets ready rolled puff pastry
   2 egg yolks
   3 teaspoons caraway seeds (or sesame seeds i preferred)
   salt to taste

Beat egg yolks and spread over three pastry sheets with a pastry brush. Sprinkle with salt to taste if desired Sprinkle caraway seeds evenly over pastry sheets. Cu each sheet in half and then each half into eight strips (1(per sheet). Place on a greased oven tray and bake in moderate oven until golden brown and crisp approximately 15–20 minutes. Store in an airtigh container. Makes 48. *Plate 20*

Note: There are usually six pastry sheets in a commercia packet of ready rolled puff pastry. You may wish to use the balance of the sheets to make more Caraway Sticks or the Herb Twists on page 46.

Caraway Sticks

The distinctive taste of caraway seeds make these Caraway Sticks delicious to serve with drinks.

Nutty Nibbles

A crunchy combination of nuts, popcorn and pretzel will delight the taste buds.

You will need:
   6 cups cooked popcorn (see recipe on page 25, usin ½ cup uncooked popcorn)
   1 cup mixed nuts
   100 g (3½ oz) pretzels (broken into smaller pieces
   50 g (1½ oz) butter
   2 tablespoons Worcestershire sauce
   1 teaspoon seasoned pepper
   ½ teaspoon garlic powder

Combine popcorn, nuts and pretzels in a bowl and mi well. Place butter, Worcestershire sauce, pepper an(garlic powder in a saucepan and simmer until butter i melted and ingredients are thoroughly mixed. Pour butte mixture over popcorn mixture and mix until all dr ingredients are well coated. Store in an airtight container. Package up in cellophane or small plastic bags tied with gift ribbon to sell. Makes approximately 8 cups (or bags).

Curried Nuts and Bolts

Men in particular seem to love this tasty curry-flavoured mixture which goes so well with a beer or two while watching sport on TV!

You will need:
    300 g (9½ oz) Nutri-Grain
    200 g (6½ oz) unsalted peanuts
    1 packet cream of chicken soup
    1 packet French onion soup
    1 teaspoon dry mustard
    2 tablespoons curry powder (more if desired)
    ½ to ⅔ cup of oil
    1 tablespoon granulated garlic (optional)

Mix cereal and nuts together well. Then mix chicken and onion soup powders, mustard and curry powder together. Stir through cereal and nuts mixture thoroughly. Heat oil until very hot and stir through mixture until dry ingredients are well coated. Store in an airtight container. Package up in cellophane or plastic bags tied with gift ribbon. Makes approximately 10 cups (or bags). *Plate 19*

Cheese Rounds

Cheese Rounds

A hint of paprika and lots of extra tasty cheese make these Cheese Rounds delicious snacks.

You will need:
    1½ cups plain flour
    1 teaspoon paprika
    ¼ teaspoon pepper
    1 teaspoon salt
    185 g (6 oz) butter
    125 g (4 oz) finely grated cheddar cheese
    2 tablespoons toasted sesame seeds
    2–3 tablespoons milk

Sift the flour and mix well with paprika, pepper and salt in a bowl. Rub butter into flour mixture. Add finely grated cheese and sesame seeds and mix in well. Moisten mixture with 2–3 tablespoons of milk. Knead lightly on a floured board and roll mixture into a long sausage shape, approximately 4 cm in diameter. Cover in plastic wrap or foil and refrigerate for at least an hour until firm. Cut into thin rounds and bake on ungreased baking trays in a moderate oven (180°C/350°F) for 10–12 minutes. Makes 60. *Plate 20*

Note: This mixture can also be rolled out thinly and cut into strips to make sesame-flavoured cheese straws. Bake as above.

Devilled Raisins

A quick and easy recipe for devilishly delicious raisins!

You will need:
  200 g (6½ oz) raisins
  1 tablespoon butter
  ½ teaspoon ginger
  ½ teaspoon salt
  sprinkle cayenne pepper

Melt butter in a saucepan, then add ginger, cayenne pepper and salt. Stir until well mixed. Then add raisins, mixing until well coated. Cook for 2–3 minutes, stirring throughout. Allow to drain on paper towel. Store in airtight jars. Package in plastic or cellophane bags. Makes 3 cups. *Plate 20*

Herb Twists

The addition of fresh herbs make these herb and cheese-flavoured twists extra savoury.

You will need:
  25 g (1 oz) butter
  3 sheets ready rolled puff pastry
  salt and pepper to taste
  ½ cup grated parmesan cheese
  ½ cup grated cheddar cheese
  3 teaspoons chopped parsley and chives

Melt butter and spread with a pastry brush over each puff pastry sheet. Sprinkle with salt and pepper to taste. Then top with parmesan cheese and tasty cheese, and fresh chopped herbs sprinkled evenly over pastry surface. Cut pastry sheet in half, and then cut each half into six equal strips. Fold each strip in half lengthwise, twist into a spiral shape, and place on a greased oven tray. Cook in a hot oven (200°C/400°F) for about ten minutes, or until golden. Makes 36. *Plate 20*

Chilli Nuts

Mexican chilli powder gives extra zing to these very tasty nuts.

You will need:
  375 g (12 oz) mixed nuts
  1 teaspoon Mexican chilli powder
  1 teaspoon all purpose seasoning
  1 teaspoon curry powder
  1 tablespoon Worcestershire sauce
  ¼ cup cooking oil

Combine chilli powder, curry powder and all purpose seasoning with the Worcestershire sauce. Pour over nuts and stir until well coated. Heat oil in a saucepan until hot, pour over nuts and stir until mixed thoroughly. Spread nuts on a tray lined with non-stick baking paper. Bake at 180°C (350°F) for 10–15 minutes or until golden brown. Cool and store in airtight containers. Package in small plastic or cellophane bags tied with gift ribbon to sell. Makes 3 cups. *Plate 19*

Pizza Popcorn

Popcorn will never taste the same after you have savoured this Italian-style version with parmesan cheese, garlic, oregano and chives.

You will need:
  2 tablespoons grated Parmesan cheese
  ¼–½ teaspoon garlic powder
  2 teaspoons dried oregano
  2 teaspoons chopped chives
  ⅓ cup oil
  ½ cup uncooked popcorn
  50 g (2 oz) butter or margarine
  2 teaspoons turmeric to colour popcorn (optional)

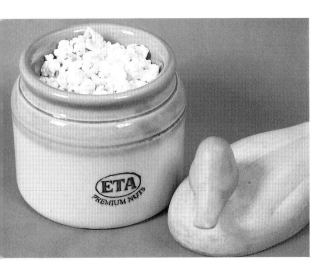

Combine grated Parmesan cheese, garlic powder, oregano and chives in a cup. Heat oil in large saucepan. Test with a few kernels of corn and when these have popped, add rest of corn and cover. Shake saucepan gently as corn pops. When popping stops, remove from heat. Melt butter or margarine and pour over popcorn, stirring popcorn to coat evenly. Quickly mix in dry ingredients thoroughly to coat (including turmeric to colour popcorn if desired). Best made the same day, but store in an airtight container, or package up in cellophane or plastic bags to sell. Makes approximately 6 cups. *Plate 19*

8. Nutty Treats

There are lots of interesting and unusual ways to use nuts in confectionery cooking, and most of them are very easy. With the wide variety of nuts available today in the average supermarket, everyone is able to eat like a gourmet with macadamias, walnuts, pistachios, peanuts, cashews, pecans and Brazil nuts being some of the favourites.

Nuts can be coated in many different flavours—from toffees to caramels, sugars to chocolate—all equally delicious! With combinations of other flavours such as coconut, coffee and ginger, they become exotic and different. Again, you are only limited by your imagination to make wonderful treats which will be highly saleable, enthusiastically received and greatly relished!

Nutty Honey Chews

Delicious honey-flavoured nut bars which can be packaged attractively for sale.

You will need:
    125 g (4 oz) butter
    ½ cup sugar
    2 tablespoons honey
    200 g (6½ oz) mixed nuts, unsalted
    chocolate to garnish (optional)

Combine butter, sugar and honey, and bring to the boil. Simmer on low for 3 to 4 minutes. Add mixed nuts and stir quickly as mixture sets almost immediately. Press into greased lamington tin and allow to set for 5–10 minutes.

Cut into finger length pieces. Decorate with drizzled chocolate if desired. Makes 12. *Plate 22*

Packaging suggestion: Cut cardboard shapes slightly larger than finger length pieces of Nutty Honey Chews and cover with foil paper. Place a Nutty Honey Chew on each cardboard shape, package in individual small plastic bags and tie with gift ribbon.

Orange Sugared Pecans

Cooking in a microwave makes Orange Sugared Pecans especially easy.

You will need:
    200 g (2 cups) pecan halves
    1 egg white, lightly beaten
    ¼ cup brown sugar
    1 tablespoon grated orange rind
    ½ teaspoon cinnamon

Place nuts in bowl and add egg white, stirring until nuts are evenly moistened. Combine remaining ingredients and sprinkle over nuts, tossing to coat evenly.

Spread nuts on shallow microwave plate and microwave uncovered on High for 4–6 minutes or until pecans lose their gloss, stirring often during cooking. Let stand until completely cool, then place in airtight container. Makes approximately 60. *Plate 22*

Sugar Coated Peanuts

Everybody likes peanuts, but they will love Sugar Coated Peanuts!

You will need:
    300 g (9½ oz) raw peanuts with red skins
    1 cup sugar
    1 cup water
    ½ teaspoon red food colouring

Combine all ingredients in a heavy frying pan. Stir over low heat until all sugar has been dissolved. Bring to boil and boil uncovered for 10 minutes. Remove from heat. Stir continually until sugar crystallises around peanuts. Spread peanuts onto a tray and allow to cool. Store in an airtight jar. Makes approximately 3 cups. *Plate 21*

Ginger Peanut Toffee

This toffee consists of a delightful combination of crystallised ginger and peanuts.

You will need:
    200 g (6½ oz) unsalted peanuts
    30 g (1 oz) crystallised ginger
    125 g (4 oz) butter
    1¼ cups sugar

⅓ cup water
2 tablespoons brown vinegar

Spread peanuts and finely chopped ginger over base of a greased lamington tin. Place butter, sugar, water and vinegar in a saucepan. Stir over low heat until butter has melted and sugar has dissolved. Bring to boil and boil uncovered for 12 to 15 minutes or until toffee reaches hard crack stage (page 19), when a small amount tested in iced water should crack. Pour mixture evenly over peanuts and ginger. Allow to set, and break into pieces. Makes approximately 30 pieces. *Plate 22*

Creamy Peanut Balls

These delightful toffee balls have a sweet creamy texture with the nutty taste of peanuts.

You will need:
    60 g (2 oz) butter
    ½ cup sugar
    1 tablespoon golden syrup
    ¾ cup sweetened condensed milk
    ½ teaspoon vanilla
    ½ cup unsalted peanuts, roughly chopped or crushed
    2 to 3 cups coconut

Combine butter, sugar and golden syrup in heavy pan. Stir mixture constantly over low heat until sugar has dissolved. Stir in sweetened condensed milk and bring to the boil, then reduce heat and simmer, stirring continually for 8 minutes or until pale golden. Add vanilla and peanuts, and mix well. Gradually mix in 2 to 3 cups of coconut until fairly stiff. Allow to cool. Take teaspoonfuls of mixture and form balls, tossing in extra coconut to coat. Refrigerate until ready for use. Makes 40. *Plate 21*

illustrated over page

Coffee Pecans

Pecans sandwiched together with a coffee filling are wonderful with after-dinner coffee.

Creamy Peanut Balls (page 49)

You will need:
    1 egg white, beaten
    1 tablespoon of strong coffee granules
    1 cup pure icing sugar
    200 g (2 cups) pecans

Add coffee to beaten egg white. Add icing sugar gradually until firm enough to mould. Roll small pieces into balls and press a ball between two pecans. Allow to set in refrigerator. Makes 40 or more. *Plate 21*

9. Fudge and Nougat Treats

Fudges and Nougats must be the most exotic and luxurious of homemade sweets, yet they are not hard to make.

Basic fudge can be flavoured with coffee, cream cheese, nuts or liqueurs, making it delicious and sophisticated enough to serve on your best silver with coffee after an intimate dinner.

Fudges and nougats are the in thing in homemade sweets. Although in the past they were cut into chunky squares, now it is popular to serve and sell them in wedges, slices or bars. Wrap in clear or light coloured cellophane to show off the delectable treat inside. Decorate bonbon style with ribbons tied at both ends, or package up in a cellophane or clear plastic bag tied up with ribbons, to make the fudge especially enticing.

Chocolate Fudge

This recipe takes 30 minutes to prepare and the chocolate makes it rich and creamy.

You will need:
    125 g (4 oz) butter
    2 tablespoons golden syrup
    400 g (1¼ cups) sweetened condensed milk
    1 cup brown sugar, firmly packed
    250 g (8 oz) dark chocolate chips

Melt butter in a saucepan and add golden syrup, sweetened condensed milk and brown sugar. Stir over a low heat until boiling. Simmer gently for 20 minutes, stirring constantly. Remove from heat. Add chocolate chips and beat until smooth. Pour mixture into a well greased bar tin. Chill. When set, cut into 10 thick slices. Alternatively, pour mixture into a 20 cm square well greased tin, and cut into 12 bars or 16 squares. *Plate 23*

Cherry Bars

Cherries, coconut, cashews and chocolate combine to make super smooth bars or squares.

Cherry Bars packaged up with Coconut Walnut Fudge (page 52)

You will need:
    375 g (12 oz) dark chocolate
    150 g (5 oz) Copha
    250 g (8 oz) glace cherries
    1 cup coconut
    250 g (8 oz) unsalted cashews

Place chopped chocolate and Copha in double boiler, stirring over simmering heat until melted. Pour one quarter of the chocolate mixture into a greased and greaseproof paper-lined slab tin.

Sprinkle cherries, coconut and cashew nuts evenly

over chocolate mixture. Remaining chocolate is poured over the top. Refrigerate until set. Cut into squares or bars using a knife dipped in hot water (and dried) for each cut. Makes 12 bars, 36 small squares or 20 larger squares. *Plate 25*

Peanut Butter Fudge

The nutty taste and texture of peanut butter gives these treats extra bite!

You will need:
    125 g (4 oz) butter
    ¾ cup crunchy peanut butter
    ½ cup liquid glucose
    1 teaspoon vanilla
    pinch salt
    2½ cups icing sugar

Beat butter until smooth. Add peanut butter, glucose, vanilla and salt, and beat until well mixed. Gradually add sifted icing sugar and continue to beat. Turn out on board and knead until smooth. Press mixture into a greased bar tin. Refrigerate, and mark into slices when firm. Store in refrigerator. Makes 12. *Plate 23*

Cream Cheese Fudge

A wonderfully smooth creamy fudge with crunchy walnuts will be a favourite treat.

You will need:
    60 g (2 oz) dark chocolate
    125 g (4 oz) cream cheese
    1 teaspoon cream
    1 teaspoon vanilla
    2 cups icing sugar
    ½ cup chopped walnuts

Melt chopped chocolate in top of double saucepan over simmering water. Remove from heat. Beat cream cheese until smooth, then add vanilla and cream. Gradually beat in sifted icing sugar, fold in melted chocolate and walnuts. Spread mixture into greased and greaseproof paper-lined square slab tin. Refrigerate until firm. Cut into squares and keep in refrigerator. Makes 16. *Plate 24*

Coconut Walnut Fudge

A super combination of chocolate, walnuts, ginger and coconut make this fudge extra special.

You will need:
    120 g (3½ oz) chocolate
    ⅓ cup walnuts, chopped
    30 g (1 oz) preserved ginger, finely chopped
    ¾ cup sweetened condensed milk
    ¾ cup coconut

Melt chocolate in double saucepan over simmering heat. Add walnuts, finely chopped ginger and sweetened condensed milk. Fold in coconut. Spread into greased and greased paper-lined bar tin. Refrigerate, cut into slices when firm and store in fridge. *Plate 25*

illustrated on previous page

52

Cherry Divinity

This is a light candy with a cherry flavour. The addition of pecans or macadamia nuts gives it a nutty crunch.

You will need:

   3 cups sugar
   ¾ cup glucose
   ¾ cup water
   2 egg whites
   3 rounded tablespoons gelatine
   1 packet glace cherries
   1 cup chopped pecans or macadamia nuts
   icing sugar for rolling cherries

Combine sugar, glucose and water in heavy saucepan. Cook over medium heat, stirring until sugar dissolves. Bring to boil, and cook to hard ball stage (130°C or 266°F) when small amount is placed in iced water.

   Meanwhile beat egg whites with an electric mixer until stiff peaks form. Beat in gelatine. When syrup reaches hard ball stage, pour in a thin stream over egg whites, beating constantly. Beat until mixture is too stiff to beat any longer with mixer.

Roll cherries in icing sugar and using a wooden spoon fold nuts and cherries into mixture. Turn into a greased 20 cm square tin and cool until firm. Cut into squares or bars with an oiled knife. Makes 25 squares. *Plate 24*

Golden Caramels

Extra chewy but delicious hard caramels are easy to make.

You will need:

   1 cup castor sugar
   90 g (3 oz) butter
   2 tablespoons golden syrup
   ⅓ cup liquid glucose
   ½ cup sweetened condensed milk
   1 teaspoon vanilla

Combine all ingredients except vanilla in a saucepan. Stir over low heat until all sugar is dissolved. Increase heat, and boil for ten minutes. Stir constantly until mixture turns dark caramel colour and reaches hard ball stage (page 19). Mix in vanilla, and pour immediately into a well greased 20 cm slab tin. Mark into squares while still hot. Allow to cool, and then break into pieces. Makes approximately 25 squares. *Plate 24*

10. Slice and Bar Treats

Slices and Bar Treats are always highly saleable at fetes and markets. Ever popular, slices can be so varied that they make a welcome and easy change to spark up our diet. Slices can be healthy, or outrageously luscious, but they are quick and easy to make and so are suitable for fundraisings.

Although there are only a few slice recipes in this chapter, if you are selling at a regular market stall, you may wish to introduce a new slice each month with your regular sweets. Using the Basic Slice recipe and varying flavourings, toppings and garnishes, this will freshen your presentation and entice your customers to come back 'to see what you have this time'. Slices and Bars are often required for catering purposes for functions and you might like to offer to supply local restaurants, coffee shops and groups.

Apricot Delight

These apricot bars flavoured with honey, sultanas and coconut really are a delight.

You will need:
- ¾ cup finely chopped dried apricots
- ½ cup water
- ½ cup honey
- ½ cup sultanas
- ½ cup desiccated coconut

⅓ cup finely chopped almonds
1 teaspoon each lemon and orange juice
1 cup powdered skim milk
1 tablespoon wheatgerm

Combine apricots and water in a large saucepan. Bring to boil and simmer until just tender. Remove from heat. Add remaining ingredients. Mix thoroughly. Spread into lightly greased 20 cm square slab tin. Refrigerate for several hours before cutting into bars. Makes 10. *Plate 28*

Walnut Slice

An easy slice with walnuts and raisins is delicious topped with lemon icing.

You will need:
- 125 g (4 oz) margarine
- 125 g (4 oz) castor sugar
- 1 tablespoon cocoa
- 250 g (8 oz) crushed Ginger Nut biscuits
- 1 egg
- ½ cup chopped walnuts
- ½ cup raisins

1 tablespoon sherry or vanilla
icing sugar, lemon flavouring or lemon juice, and
walnut pieces to garnish (optional)

Melt margarine in saucepan over medium heat. Add
sugar, stirring until dissolved. Boil, stirring until light and
creamy (approximately 2 minutes). Remove from heat,
then add cocoa, crushed biscuit crumbs, beaten egg,
walnuts, raisins and sherry. Mix well. Press into greased
20 cm square slab tin. Allow to cool. Ice with lemon icing
if desired, cut into squares, and top each square with a
piece of walnut to garnish. Makes 16. *Plate 28*

Cocoa Peanut Logs

Quick and easy peanut logs made with Coco Pops,
peanut butter and chocolate have great appeal to
children.

You will need:
185 g (6 oz) chocolate
⅓ cup peanut butter
4 cups Coco Pops (or Rice Bubbles)

Melt chocolate in a saucepan over simmering water. Stir
in peanut butter, and then mix in Coco Pops or Rice
Bubbles. Press mixture into a greased 20 cm square slab
tin, and allow to cool. Cut into logs. Makes 10. *Plate 28*

Sesame Honey Fingers

Sesame Honey Fingers

Another quick and easy recipe with the flavour of honey
and sesame seeds.

You will need:
½ cup margarine
½ cup brown sugar
3 tablespoons honey
4 cups Rice Bubbles
⅓ cup sesame seeds

Combine honey, margarine and brown sugar in a large
saucepan. Bring to boil. Cook over low heat for three
minutes, stirring constantly. Remove from heat and add
Rice Bubbles and sesame seeds. Press into a greased
20 cm square slab tin. Allow to cool, and cut into fingers.
Makes 14. *Plate 28*

Basic Slice

This slice is very simple and easy, can be varied in as
many ways as you can think of, and is delicious.

You will need:
1 cup self raising flour
½ cup sugar
½ cup coconut
125 g (4 oz) margarine

Mix dry ingredients. Melt margarine, pour into dry
ingredients and mix well. Press into lamington tin. Bake
in moderate oven for approximately 15 minutes until
nicely browned on top.

Chocolate Topping
1 cup icing sugar
2 dessertspoons cocoa
3 tablespoons sweetened condensed milk
1 teaspoon vanilla
1 cup coconut
walnut-sized knob of butter or margarine
milk to thin to thick paste consistency

Mix all ingredients well. Spread over slice. Cut into
squares. Makes 20. *Plate 27*

Note: Vary topping with different flavourings such as
lemon juice or grated orange rind.

Illustrated on next page

55

Basic Slice (page 55) in foreground, with Macadamia Slice

Macadamia Slice

Using macadamia nuts for flavour, a rich butter icing and crushed macadamia nuts as a garnish, this is a super slice!

You will need:
   1 cup self raising flour
   ½ cup sugar
   ½ cup coconut
   ½ cup halved macadamia nuts
   150 g (5 oz) margarine

Mix dry ingredients. Melt margarine, pour into dry ingredients and mix well. Press into lamington tin. Bake in moderate oven for approximately 15 minutes until nicely browned on top.

Butter Icing
   2 cups icing sugar
   2 large tablespoons soft butter or margarine
   1 dessertspoon vanilla
   milk to thin to thick paste consistency
   crushed macadamia nuts for topping

Mix icing sugar, butter and vanilla well. Add milk to thin to thick paste consistency. Spread over slice and sprinkle crushed macadamia nuts as a garnish. Cut into squares. Makes 20. *Plate 27*

Sultana Slice

Another equally delicious slice using wholemeal flour and sultanas with the delightful tang of lemon icing.

You will need:
   1 cup wholemeal self raising flour
   ½ cup brown sugar
   ½ cup coconut (or muesli, rolled oats or bran)
   ½ cup sultanas (or dates, walnuts or dried apricots)
   150 g (5 oz) margarine

Mix dry ingredients. Melt margarine, pour onto dry ingredients and mix well. Press into lamington tin. Bake in moderate oven for approximately 15 minutes until nicely browned on top. If you want a soft cake-like texture rather than a biscuity texture, add an egg to the mixture.

Lemon Icing
   2 cups icing sugar
   2 large tablespoons soft butter or margarine
   3–4 tablespoons lemon juice
   coconut for garnish

Mix icing sugar, butter or margarine and lemon juice well, until a thick paste consistency. Spread over slice, and sprinkle coconut over as a garnish. Cut into squares. Makes 20. *Plate 27*

Marshmallow Slice

A quick and easy Marshmallow Slice which can be varied with different colourings and flavourings.

You will need:
   1½ cups coconut
   1½ cups self raising flour
   ½ cup brown sugar
   125 g (4 oz) margarine

23

Plate 23: Peanut Butter Fudge (p.52) and Chocolate Fudge (p.51)

FUDGE TREATS

Plate 24 (clockwise from top left): Cherry Divinity (p.53), Cream Cheese Fudge (p.52) and Golden Caramels (p.53)

Plate 25: Coconut Walnut Fudge (p.52) and Cherry Bars (p.51) packaged in a basket

24

25

Plate 26: Caramel Slice (p.61) and Marshmallow Slice (p.56)

Plate 27: Basic Slice, Sultana Slice and Macadamia Slice (p.56)

SLICE TREATS

Plate 28 (from left): Cocoa Peanut Logs (p.55), Sesame Honey Fingers (p.55), Walnut Slice (p.54) and Apricot Delight (p.54)

Plate 29 (left to right): Fruit Cake Rum Balls (p.63), Christmas Crunch (p.63), Santa's Special Buttons (p.62) and Christmas Logs (p.64) wrapped in cellophane

Plate 30 (left to right): Christmas Parcels (p.65), Mini Christmas Puddings (p.64), Mini Christmas Cakes (p.64) and White Christmas (p.62)

CELEBRATION TREATS

Plate 31: Easter Bonnets (p.65) on stand, Chocolate Easter Eggs (p.66) made with white chocolate and Liqueur Easter Eggs (p.66)

32

33

Plate 32 (clockwise from bottom left): Packaged Gingerbread Men, Funny Faces and Smartie Squares on coloured plastic plates in bags, Marshmallow in catering wine glass, covered yoghurt container, cardboard basket, tin covered with wallpaper, crepe paper flowers, crepe paper carrots, cardboard basket with Strawberries, gift bag

Plate 33 (clockwise from left): Crepe paper flower, takeaway plastic container, recycled jars with fabric toppers, cardboard basket, packaged Gingerbread Men, crepe paper umbrella

PACKAGING IDEAS
(pages 31–33)

Plate 34 (clockwise from bottom left): Cardboard baskets, covered box lid with paper doily insert, crepe paper bon bons with motifs, yoghurt container covered with gift paper, biscuit tin with cut-out motifs glued to front containing treats packaged in small plastic bags tied with gift ribbon

34

Mix all dry ingredients together. Pour on melted margarine and mix well. Press into a lamington tin. Bake at 180°C (350°F) for 15 minutes until lightly browned. Allow to cool.

Marshmallow Topping
- 1¼ cups castor sugar
- 1 tablespoon gelatine
- 1 cup boiling water

Stir gelatine into boiling water until dissolved. Pour onto sugar in a bowl and beat with an electric mixer until thick. Spread over base and set in fridge. Cut into squares. Makes 24. *Plate 26*

Variations: Marshmallow can be coloured with a few drops of food colouring well blended through the mixture. Flavouring essences (peppermint, lemon, etc.) can be used by adding a few drops when beating mixture. You can also use a tablespoon of instant coffee or the pulp of two passionfruit for a totally different look and flavour.

Caramel Slice

A rich caramel-topped slice is great to serve with coffee or tea.

You will need:
- ½ cup plain flour
- ½ cup self raising flour
- ½ cup brown sugar
- 1 cup coconut
- 125 g (4 oz) butter

Sift flours together in a bowl, and add sugar and coconut. Melt butter and mix all ingredients together. Press mixture into a well greased lamington tray. Bake in a moderate oven for 15 minutes until lightly browned.

Caramel Topping
- 400 g (1¼ cups) sweetened condensed milk
- 2 tablespoons golden syrup
- 2 teaspoons butter

Melt all ingredients together over low heat, stirring for a few minutes until well mixed. Spread topping over base and bake for another 15 minutes. Allow to cool.

Chocolate Icing
- 100 g (3½ oz) cooking chocolate
- 2 teaspoons butter

Melt chocolate and butter over simmering water in a double saucepan. When base and caramel topping have cooled, spread with chocolate icing. Cut into squares when set. Makes 24. *Plate 26*

11. Celebration Treats

At Christmas or Easter time, or any other special occasion, virtually any sweet can be used. It is the way it is presented, packaged and given that makes it special. The message and traditions of the occasion are important and you can present your sweets accordingly.

Christmas is a wonderful time to share extra special treats, and even the most ordinary sweet can be decorated, coloured or garnished in the traditional colours of red, white and green. The making, packaging and presenting of Easy Treats can be a family affair, as children love to be included in the mixing, measuring and garnishing of sweets. People always appreciate a homemade gift that you have taken the time and trouble to prepare just for them!

Eastertime has become very commercial, and children love the idea of sweets and Easter eggs, but we should not forget the traditional meaning of Easter, and celebrate accordingly.

Children's birthdays are a good time to indulge in all kinds of brightly decorated sweets and special treats. Involve the kids in the making of the goodies, and they will be especially thrilled.

Mother's Day and Father's Day are also good times to package up and present sweets. Children think it is wonderful to be able to make something themselves to give to mums and dads on their special day. Many of the sweets in this book are simple enough for children to make. A class project could involve children, under supervision, helping to make sweets for their school fete, or for Mother's Day or Father's Day stalls as fundraisers.

Easy Treats can be made at any time to have on hand in the event that guests drop by unexpectedly, or to have a special treat to serve with the after-dinner coffee. Make every day a special occasion!

You will need:
    40 g (1¼ oz) Copha
    1 egg white
    2⅓ cups icing sugar, sifted
    1 teaspoon lemon juice
    3–4 drops green food colouring
    36 red glace cherry halves or pecan or walnut halve:

Melt Copha in a saucepan over low heat. Mix togethe egg white, sifted icing sugar, lemon juice, melted Coph; and green food colouring until well blended and ther knead until smooth. Shape into small balls and place or a foil-lined baking tray. Place half a glace cherry, walnu or pecan on the middle of each ball and press down tc make a button shape. Refrigerate to set. Makes 36
Plate 29

Santa's Special Buttons

Kids will think these edible buttons are just great, especially with the cherries in the middle!

White Christmas

An old favourite that can really get into the Christma spirit, especially if coloured red and green.

You will need:
    1 cup Rice Bubbles
    1 cup mixed fruit
    1 cup icing sugar
    1 cup powdered milk
    1 cup coconut
    ½ cup chopped glace cherries
    250 g (8 oz) Copha
    3-4 drops of red and green food colouring (optional)

Melt Copha over low heat in a saucepan. Mix all dry ingredients and combine with melted Copha. (Colour with red or green food colouring for added interest.) Spread into a lamington tin and allow to set. Cut into squares and keep under refrigeration. Makes 14 bars or 24 squares. *Plate 30*

Fruit Cake Rum Balls

An unusual way to use up left-over fruit cake makes delectable rum balls.

You will need:
    2½ cups crumbled fruit cake
    1 tablespoon rum
    50 g (1½ oz) melted Copha
    1 tablespoon cocoa
    coconut or sprinkles to coat

Melt Copha over low heat in a saucepan. Combine all ingredients thoroughly with melted Copha. Roll into balls, and toss in coconut or chocolate sprinkles. Refrigerate to store. Makes 20 large or 30 small balls. *Plate 29*

Christmas Crunch

Brazil nuts make these Christmas treats extra crunchy.

You will need:
    125 g (4 oz) Copha
    200 g (6½ oz) Brazil nut chocolate
    250 g (8 oz) shortbread biscuits, crushed
    125 g (4 oz) Brazil nuts, chopped
    2 egg whites, lightly beaten

Melt Brazil nut chocolate and Copha in a double saucepan over simmering water. Mix biscuit crumbs, Brazil nuts, egg whites into melted chocolate mixture until well blended. Take a teaspoonful of mixture at a time, squeeze into shape and roll into balls. Place in small confectionery cases if desired. Allow to set in the refrigerator. Makes 48. *Plate 29*

Mini Christmas Puddings

Mini Christmas Puddings tied up in calico look just like the real thing, but are even more delicious.

You will need:
  3 cups brown sugar
  1 cup boiling water
  1 tablespoon vinegar
  ¼ teaspoon cinnamon
  2 cups mixed fruit and nuts
  ¼ cup coconut

In a heavy saucepan, stir 3 cups of brown sugar with boiling water and vinegar. Keep stirring over moderate heat until sugar is dissolved. Bring to the boil, and boil until just at the soft ball stage. Remove from heat. Beat in cinnamon, mixed fruit and nuts and coconut. Drop mixture onto non-stick baking paper, forming into large balls with two spoons. Set in the refrigerator. Makes 12 large balls.

When hardened, wrap in 20 cm squares of muslin with pinked edges, tie with red and/or green gift ribbon, and decorate with a small sprig of holly.

Alternatively, holly leaves can be cut from green cardboard, holes punched in one end, and threaded onto the ribbon before tying. Colour in red holly berries on the leaves with a red Texta pen or screw up small pieces of red cellophane to make berries and glue in place on holly leaves. *Plate 30*

Christmas Logs

Christmas Logs make colourful tree decorations or small gifts on each plate at your Christmas table, with their bright wrappers and ribbon ties.

You will need:
  150 g (5 oz) Copha
  ½ cup brown sugar
  2 cups crushed Milk Coffee biscuits
  1 tablespoon cocoa
  200 g (6½ oz) Hawaiian mix of nuts, glace fruit, etc
  3 tablespoons orange juice
  1 tablespoon coffee essence
  foil wrapping paper or cellophane and gift ribbon (optional)

Melt Copha in a saucepan over low heat. Mix brown sugar, biscuit crumbs, cocoa, mixed nuts and glace fruit, orange juice and coffee essence with melted Copha and blend well. Press into greased and baking paper-lined lamington tin and allow to cool. Cut into fingers. Wrap bonbon style in bright foil wrapping paper or coloured cellophane approximately 15 cm long, and secure each end with coloured gift ribbon with the ends curled. Makes about 22 fingers. *Plate 29*

Mini Christmas Cakes

These delightful little boiled fruit cakes can be decorated for Christmas with icing, green leaves and red berries made from Mint Leaves and Smarties.

You will need:
  250 g (8 oz) sultanas
  125 g (4 oz) cooking margarine
  1 cup water
  1 cup brown sugar
  1 teaspoon bicarbonate of soda
  1 teaspoon mixed spices
  2 eggs

2 cups self raising flour
1 tablespoon sherry
patty pans
icing sugar, Mint Leaves and red Smarties for
    decoration (optional)

Melt margarine in a large saucepan. Add sultanas, water, brown sugar, bicarbonate of soda and mixed spices and boil for five minutes. Allow mixture to cool and then add well beaten eggs, self raising flour and sherry and mix well. Place in patty papers and cook in a moderate oven for 30 minutes.

Decorate with white icing, 2 Mint Leaves and a red Smartie. Makes 24. *Plate 30*

Christmas Parcels

Using purchased marzipan, mini parcels can be coloured, shaped and decorated with gift ribbons, and are sure to delight the kids!

You will need:
    200 g (6½ oz) marzipan
    food colourings
    coloured gift ribbon

Divide marzipan into several sections and use a few drops of food colouring to colour each section differently. Knead well until colour is well mixed and shape marzipan into various sizes and shapes for mini parcels. Allow to dry thoroughly on a tray. Then tie up each parcel exactly as you would a real parcel, using gift ribbon with the ends curled attractively. Makes about 20 parcels, depending on size. *Plate 30*

Easter Bonnets

This is a cute idea for a market stall at Easter time, or for surprise treats for children at birthday parties.

You will need:
    2 cups icing sugar
    2 egg whites
    250 g (8 oz) round sweet biscuits
    packet of medium sized marshmallows
    food colouring
    piping bag and attachments

Blend icing sugar with egg whites until stiff and smooth. Spread icing mixture on top of each biscuit for the hat brim, and push a marshmallow into the middle of each one to make a hat crown. Divide remainder of icing mixture into several dishes and put a few drops of different food colouring in each dish. Blend icing until colours are well mixed. Place coloured icing in piping bag and using different attachments pipe around the crown of the hat, making flower shapes, bows, et cetera as shown in the photograph. Makes about 30, depending on number of biscuits in packet. *Plate 31*

65

Chocolate Easter Eggs

Colourful little Easter eggs can be displayed in handmade cardboard baskets or boxes.

You will need:
  100 g (3½ oz) white chocolate
  ½ cup dried apricots, finely chopped
  100 g (3½ oz) chopped nuts
  1½ cups cake crumbs
  1 tablespoon sherry
  1 tablespoon apricot jam
  300 g (9½ oz) white chocolate
  100s and 1000s, crushed nuts or chocolate sprinkles
     for garnish

Melt 100 g (3½ oz) white chocolate over simmering hot water. Combine with apricots, nuts, cake crumbs, sherry and apricot jam until well mixed. Take teaspoonfuls of mixture, roll into balls, and shape into egg shapes. Allow to set in refrigerator. When hard, melt 300 g (9½ oz) white chocolate, dip eggs in to coat, and set on tray lined with non-stick baking paper. Sprinkle with 100s and 1000s, crushed nuts or chocolate sprinkles to garnish. Allow to set in refrigerator. Place in small foil or paper patty cases and present in a handmade cardboard basket or box. Makes about 30 eggs. *Plate 31*

Liqueur Easter Eggs

These rich eggs can be flavoured with your favourite liqueurs to make them deliciously exotic.

You will need:
  200 g (6½ oz) marzipan
  1 tablespoon liqueur
  icing sugar to knead marzipan and keep hands
     unsticky
  100 g (3½ oz) chocolate
  25 g (1 oz) Copha

Chop marzipan up in a bowl. Add liqueur and let marzipan soak it up for a few minutes. Knead into a ball, dusting hands and marzipan with extra icing sugar to keep from sticking. Roll into small balls, then mould them into egg shapes. Allow to set in fridge. When hard, melt Copha and chocolate, dip eggs in to coat, and allow to dry on a non-stick baking paper-lined tray in the refrigerator. Put into small foil or paper patty cases and present in a decorated box or basket if desired. Makes about 35 small eggs. *Plate 31*

Index

(Numbers in *italics* are colour plate references)

Apricot Ambrosia, 13, *1*
Apricot Delight, 54, *28*
Apricot Rounds, 41, *16*
Apricot Surprises, 28, *10*

Barley Sugar, 20, *9*
Basic Dipping Mix, 11
Basic Slice, 55, *27*
Bubbly Marshmallows, 17, *6*
Butterscotch, 20, *9*

Candied Peel, 43, *17*
Candy Popcorn, 26, *8, 9*
Caramel Popcorn, 26, *9*
Caramel Slice, 61, *26*
Caraway Sticks, 44, *20*
Carrot Candies, 41, *18*
Celebration treats, 62–6
Cereal Cases, 16, *6*
Cereal treats, 15–18
Cheese Rounds, 45, *20*
Cherry Bars, 51, *25*
Cherry Coconut Bars, 17, *6*
Cherry Divinity, 53, *24*
Chilli Nuts, 46, *19*
Chocolate Cherries, 11, *2*
Chocolate Crackles, 27, *8*
Chocolate Easter Eggs, 66, *31*
Chocolate Fudge, 51, *23*
Chocolate Ginger, 12, *4*
Chocolate Prunes with Port, 12, *1*
Chocolate Roughs, 16, *6*
Chocolate Spiders, 13, *1*
Chocolate treats, 11–14
Christmas Crunch, 63, *29*
Christmas Logs, 64, *29*
Christmas Parcels, 65, *30*
Cocoa Peanut Logs, 55, *28*
Coconut Ice, 26, *9*
Coconut Walnut Fudge, 52, *25*
Coffee Pecans, 50, *21*
Conversion tables, 10
Cream Cheese Fudge, 52, *24*

Creamy Peanut Balls, 49, *21*
Curried Nuts and Bolts, 45, *19*

Date Slices, 42, *16*
Devilled Raisins, 45, *20*

Easter Bonnets, 65, *31*
Easy Homemade Chocolates, 12, *1*
Easy Rocky Road, 28, *12*
Edible Animals, 34, *14*

Favourite treats, 19–27
French Chocolates, 14, *3*
Fruity Frosts, 13, *1*
Fudge and nougat treats, 51–3
Funny Faces, 36, *13*
Fruit Cake Rum Balls, 63, *29*

Gingerbread Men, 36, *15*
Ginger Peanut Toffee, 49, *22*
Golden Caramels, 53, *24*

Herb Twists, 46, *20*
Honey Bubble Crunch, 15, *5*
Honeycomb, 27
Honey Joys, 18, *7*

Introduction, 7

Kids' treats, 31–6

Liqueur Easter Eggs, 66, *31*

Macadamia Slice, 56, *27*
Marshmallow, 35
Marshmallow Cones, 35, *13*
Marshmallow Cups, 35, *13*
Marshmallow Slice, 56, *26*
Marzipan Animals and Shapes, 35, *15*
Marzipan Log, 29, *10*
Mini Christmas Cakes, 64, *30*
Mini Christmas Puddings, 64, *30*
Moonshine Biffs, 28, *11*

Muesli Bars, 42, *18*
Muesli Munchies, 43, *16*

Nutty Honey Chews, 48, *22*
Nutty Nibbles, 44
Nutty treats, 48–50

Orange Sugared Pecans, 48, *22*

Packaging and presentation, 8
Packaging ideas, 31, *32, 33, 34*
Peanut Butter Balls, 29, *11*
Peanut Butter Fudge, 52, *23*
Peanut Butter Squares, 43, *18*
Pine Nut Toffees, 30, *12*
Pink Mallow Bars, 17, *5*
Pizza Popcorn, 46, *19*
Popcorn—Basic Recipe, 25

Santa's Special Buttons, 62, *29*
Savoury treats, 44–6
School Toffees, 20, *8*
Sesame Caramel Toffee, 30, *12*
Sesame Honey Fingers, 55, *28*
Sesame Snaps, 30, *12*
Sherbet, 27, *8*
Slice and bar treats, 54–61
Smartie Squares, 36, *13*
Snack treats, 41–3
Strawberries, 34, *15*
Sugar Coated Peanuts, 49, *21*
Sultana Slice, 56, *27*
Sweet treats, 28–30

Toffee Apples, 25, *9*
Toffee and Toffee Testing, 19
Truccles, 34, *14*

Umbrella Toffees, 20, *8*

Walnut Slice, 54, *28*
Weet-Bix Kids, 15, *5*
White Christmas, 62, *30*